VITAL ISSUES OF THE CONSTITUTION

Robert H. Ratcliffe, Ph.D.
Vice President
Lewis & Clark Community College
Godfrey, Illinois

Irving Gordon, J.D.
Professor of Law
Northwestern University
Evanston, Illinois

E. Walter Miles, Ph.D.
San Diego State University
San Diego, California

HOUGHTON MIFFLIN COMPANY **Boston**

Atlanta Dallas Geneva, Illinois Palo Alto Princeton Toronto

Printed in the U.S.A.
ISBN: 0-395-48340-9
EFGHIJ-B-9876543

ACKNOWLEDGMENTS

The materials in this series were developed by the Law in American Society Foundation. Funds were made available under Title I of the Elementary and Secondary Education Act of 1965. All units benefited from the contributions of the authors listed below as well as the many elementary and high school teachers who have participated in the Foundation's summer institutes.

LAW IN AMERICAN SOCIETY BOARD OF DIRECTORS

President

Perry L. Fuller

Attorney

Hinshaw, Culbertson, Moelmann, Hoban & Fuller (Chicago)

Thomas J. Boodell, Jr., attorney, Keck, Mahin & Cate (Chicago); **Alex Elson,** attorney, Rosenthal & Schanfield (Chicago); **Margaret Fallers,** Associate Provost, University of Chicago; **The Honorable Joan B. Gottschall,** U.S. District Court, Chicago; **Ted B. Lewis,** attorney, Lewis, Kappes, Fuller & Eads, Indianapolis; **E. Walter Miles,** Professor of Political Science, San Diego State University; **Karen E. O'Neil,** Charlottesville, Virginia; **Reverend John T. Richardson,** President, DePaul University, Chicago; **Peter R. Senn,** Professor Emeritus, City Colleges of Chicago.

Contributing authors to *Vital Issues of the Constitution:*

M. Cherif Bassiouni, Professor of Law, DePaul University, Chicago; **Shirley L. Baugher; Richard F. Bonas,** Old Orchard Junior High School, Skokie, Illinois; **Thomas J. Boodell, Jr.,** attorney; **Robert E. Burns,** Professor of Law, DePaul University, Chicago; **Basil Condos,** attorney; **Philip Dreyer; Lee Ehman; Richard Ellis; Arlene F. Gallagher,** Social Studies Consultant, Southborough, Massachusetts; **William Gibson,** attorney; **Rita Goldman; Richard C. Groll,** former Dean of Law, DePaul University, Chicago; **Peter R. Kolker,** attorney; **Michael Lawrence,** attorney; **John R. Lee,** former Professor of Education, Northwestern University; **Timothy H. Little,** Professor, School of Education, Michigan State University; **Thomas Newman; Robert O'Neil,** President, University of Virginia; **Mary Jane O'Shea; William S. Peters,** Professor of Education, St. Xavier College, Chicago; **Charles Quigley; Honorable Stephen Schiller; Raymond Starr,** Professor of History, San Diego State University; **Isidore Starr,** Former President of the National Council for the Social Studies; **Leigh Taylor,** attorney; **Jack Zevin,** Professor, Department of Education, Queens College, New York.

FOREWORD

Today's students are restless and independent. Growing up in an uncertain world, they strive to discover and do "their own thing," to work out their own code of behavior. They reject dogmatism. Today's students want to investigate true-to-life problems relevant to their own world. In solving problems, they are likely to put their trust in experience as a teacher—both concrete experience personally encountered and experience vicariously derived from the omnipresent communications media.

The methodology of the law, the case method, ideally meets the needs of today's young Americans exploring social problems. For, as Justice Oliver Wendell Holmes said, "The life of the law has not been logic: it has been experience." Logic is an exact mode of inquiry well suited to mathematics. It is less suited to the law, which deals with human conflicts, each tending to be special, urgent, fogged with contradictions, entangled in a web of changing times and circumstances. The law proceeds from case to case. A case, however, is not just an economic problem, or a sociological problem, or a political problem; typically it is a complex of problems touching on several of these aspects.

The law's mode of inquiry is to analyze the complex of facts, sift out the key issues, and apply a rule that seems applicable under the circumstances. Our rules of law are not exotic and abstract; they are based on the common, experimental, interdisciplinary wisdom of American legislators and jurists. Our rules of law are simply the values which our American society has selected as important enough to enforce. The law, basically, is a powerful tool for settling real-life conflicts.

VITAL ISSUES OF THE CONSTITUTION is a book which can significantly enrich basic courses in civics, government, political science, and problems of democracy. It was primarily designed, however, to provide a focus of legal concepts for an American history course.

The book deals with key cases of constitutional law. In them, the student finds the landmark tenets of our heritage, a code of national values including such things as freedom of belief, freedom of expression, equal opportunity, federal control of interstate commerce, fair trial. Chosen against the criteria of contemporary relevance and historical representativeness, these cases enable the student to grapple with the great unsettled issues of our time and to understand how these enduring problems have been treated throughout our history.

In each case, students dig into the pivotal issues of our nation's history. Since this phased program provides progressively greater comparison of earlier constitutional cases with contemporary ones, students become keenly aware of the law's growth and of history's relevance today. Thus, the book goes far beyond the traditional "Bill of Rights" units. These all too often have been limited to theoretical outlines of civil liberties as they appeared in the Constitution and its amendments or, on the other hand, show such liberties only as contemporary problems, thus denying the student a chance to see the dynamic evolution of values basic to our heritage.

VITAL ISSUES OF THE CONSTITUTION, stressing issues rather than rules and institutions, shows our legal system in actual, dynamic, sometimes controversial operation. The Law in American Society Foundation, in cooperation with the Chicago Bar Association and the Chicago Board of Education, developed these materials over a three-year period. An interdisciplinary team of lawyers, law professors, political scientists, educators, and master teachers has woven the critical-thinking approach into every chapter. The learner moves through these pages as an articulate participant, a decision-maker. The case studies are nontechnical and excitingly readable. Questions and activities build skills in analysis, synthesis, and evaluation. Discovery techniques are even used to explore the dramatic, realistic, and highly motivating illustrations.

This program has been classroom-tested with some 50,000 students. These students showed a remarkable growth in learning—not only in what they knew about America's history and America's laws, but also in how they felt about both. The materials had an obvious positive effect on student attitudes about our constitutional system. This remains a fundamental goal of the program—to lead today's students to: (1) an acceptance of value conflict as a normal facet of our pluralistic society and (2) a commitment to reason and compromise, through the process of justice, as the best and sanest way to resolve conflict in the dangerous world ahead.

PERRY L. FULLER
President
Law in American Society Foundation

CONTENTS

INTRODUCTION: Constitution, Court, and Legal System

Spring had come again to Columbia, South Carolina. This year, however, the seeds of racial strife were sprouting. Late on a March morning, almost 200 demonstrators—including both high-school and college students—gathered at the Zion Baptist Church. The South Carolina General Assembly was in session at the old State House. And the students were determined to march over there and give the legislators a piece of their mind—to outline "the present conditions of discriminatory actions against blacks." The hour neared noon.

Tension mounted among the students. Then, on signal, they headed out—stepping along in orderly groups of roughly fifteen.

Blocks away, around the State House, a pre-Civil War landmark, law officers stood waiting. Authorities had been warned that the demonstrators were coming. Fifteen Columbia police officers were stationed on the State House grounds, an area of two city blocks open to the public. In addition, there were a dozen state officers and a few deputy sheriffs.

The marchers entered the grounds through the horseshoe drive. They carried placards that made their position crystal clear. *Down with discrimination!* Single file, sometimes two abreast, the young blacks marched around the State House grounds for half an hour. Orderly. Peacefully. A crowd of curiosity-seekers gathered. Some said 200; others, 300.

Despite the activity, no vehicles were prevented from entering or leaving the horseshoe drive and parking area. Traffic was slowed a bit at a nearby intersection. But an officer dispatched to the scene kept the cars moving.

The crowd of onlookers made no hostile remarks or gestures. The Columbia city manager, however, said he spied among them a few "possible troublemakers." He felt that "a dangerous situation was really building up."

Police told the protesters to break up in fifteen minutes—or be arrested. The students ignored the order. Stamping their feet, clapping their hands, they sang "The Star-Spangled Banner" and "We Shall Not Be Moved." A placard saying *You can jail our bodies but not our souls* was raised. The city manager said the demonstrators listened to a "religious harangue" from one of their leaders and became "boisterous" and "loud."

As soon as fifteen minutes expired, police moved in. They arrested 187 demonstrators and marched them off to jail.

Columbia authorities claimed that the demonstrators had violated the state "breach of peace" law and should be punished. Under South Carolina law, breach of peace was defined as follows: "A violation of public order, a disturbance of the public tranquility, by any act or conduct inciting to violence. . . . It is not necessary that the peace be actually broken. . . . Nor is actual personal violence an essential element in the offense."

The arrested demonstrators claimed that the state had violated their constitutional rights to free speech, to free assembly, and to petition for redress of grievances.

Illustration Analysis

Analyze the pictures on the preceding pages. Which elements, if any, in this design relate to the Constitution? Which elements, if any, relate to the Supreme Court? What message, if any, is communicated by the way these elements are interrelated in this composition?

IN YOUR OPINION

1. What kind of institution, if any, should settle the legal dispute between the state and the demonstrators?
2. What kind of procedure or steps are used to settle such disputes under the American system of law? Usually, who are the parties to such a dispute?

3. Who normally decides the facts of a legal case? Who decides what law applies to the case? Was this case a civil case or a criminal case? What's the difference?
4. If a mistake in the law is made in settling the case, how can the injured party get it corrected?
5. What are laws? Why does America have a system of law? What are the roots of the American system of law?
6. What is a constitution? What is a statute? What is the basic constitutional issue in the above case? What institution under the American system of law has the final word in settling such an issue? How do you think this case was finally settled? Why?

ANATOMY OF A TRIAL

Trial of the 187 demonstrators took place in a Columbia, South Carolina, court. They were convicted of a breach of the peace. Under our system of law, a **trial** is an official hearing that examines the legal issues between the parties. This particular trial was a **criminal case,** that is, one initiated by society or the government against a private person or group. The **defendant** is the party accused of committing a crime—an offense against society that injures a person (such as assault) or property (such as burglary). And the **prosecuting attorney** is the official who prosecutes, or conducts, the legal action against the defendant in the name of state, or government. For its trial, this case was officially entitled *South Carolina v. Edwards.* Edwards is the last name of one of the defendants in the case.

The other major category of legal action in our system is the **civil case.** It involves a legal dispute between two or more private persons or groups. Typical examples include: the breaking of a contract, or legal agreement between two or more parties; the trespass by one person on the property of another; or an automobile accident caused by the negligence of a driver. The party initiating the action, the party asking the court to grant a remedy for some violation of his or her rights, is the **plaintiff.** As in the criminal case, the party against whom the **lawsuit,** or legal action, is brought is the defendant.

The function of a trial is to sift the truth from a mass of contradictory evidence, and to do so the fact-finding tribunal must hear both truthful and false witnesses.

— Justice Black, *In re Michael* (1945)

JUDGE AND JURY

In both criminal and civil trials, the role of the **judge,** in general, is to determine what laws apply to the case. Using certain rules of **procedure** to conduct the trial in an orderly fashion, the judge decides how and when each party may present evidence. This may include physical objects, records, and documents, but normally it consists mainly of **testimony,** or oral statements, given by a party and his or her witnesses. The role of the **jury,** typically twelve members, is to sift all the evidence presented and decide what the facts are.

VERDICTS AND JUDGMENTS

After both parties have presented all their evidence, the judge **instructs** the jury. That is, the judge advises them what laws might apply to the given set of circumstances. Then the jury **retires:** they seclude themselves to weigh the evidence. Their **verdict** is their decision on the criminal guilt or civil liability of the defendant. Based on the verdict, the judge issues his or her **judgment**—an official determination of the case—ordering that certain acts be done by one or both parties. The judge might order, for instance, a defendant in a civil case to pay money damages to the plaintiff in order to make amends for an injury already done. And in some cases, the judge may grant the plaintiff an **injunction,** a court order forbidding the defendant to do a threatened harmful act or to stop such an act already in progress. In a criminal case, the judge hands down a sentence that punishes the convicted defendant for his or her offense against society. It normally calls for a money fine or a period of imprisonment, or both. For example, in the *Edwards* case, the judge issued sentences for the 187 defendants that ranged from a \$10 fine or 5 days in jail to a \$100 fine or 30 days in jail.

RIGHT TO APPEAL

Trial courts search for truth and appellate courts search for error.

— Anonymous

In this, as well as in other cases, criminal and civil, a party can generally make an **appeal** when he or she believes: (1) that the judge made an error in conducting a trial, and (2) that the error hurt this party's position in the trial. An appeal allows such a party to ask the judges of a higher court to review the trial. There is no jury in an "appellate" court. Appellate judges: (1) review the written **record** of the trial proceedings, (2) read **briefs,** or written arguments, presented by the attorneys for both sides, and (3) listen in court to their **oral arguments.** The main question is whether an error was made at the trial that unjustly prejudiced a party's case. The decision reached by the appellate court may affirm the trial judgment, reverse it, or order a new trial. And, in a written opinion, the higher court usually outlines the legal reasoning behind its ruling.

Judicial review gives time for the sober second thought.

— Justice Douglas, *We the Judges* (1955)

The defendants in the *Edwards* case appealed first to the Supreme Court of South Carolina, which affirmed the judgment of the trial court. The defendants next got the case reviewed by the United States Supreme Court. By now, at the highest court in our system, the case title had been turned around (*Edwards v. South Carolina,* 1963)—the first-named party being the one who sought the review.

Reversing the rulings of the state courts, the high bench found in favor of the appellant. It agreed with the 187 students that South Carolina had violated their rights, under the Constitution, "of free speech, free assembly, and freedom to petition for redress of their grievances." There had been no violence, said the Court, nor any threat of violence. Police protection was sufficient.

The "breach of peace" law was too vague and general. "And they were convicted," said the Court's opinion, "upon evidence which showed no more than that the opinions which they were peaceably expressing were sufficiently opposed to the views of the majority of the community to attract a crowd and necessitate police protection."

EVOLUTION OF A LEGAL SYSTEM

What is a constitution? What is a law? How did the American system of law evolve? What role does the U.S. Supreme Court serve in this system? These and other fundamental background questions should be examined briefly before plunging into the vital issues raised in this book.

FEDERAL COURT SYSTEM

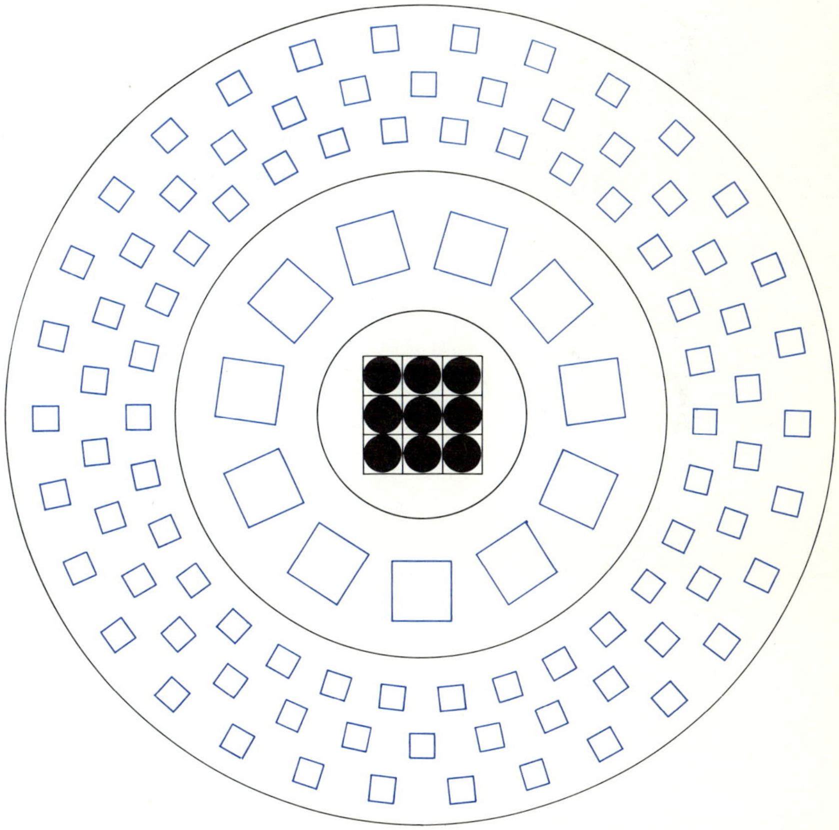

Roughly 90 U.S. District Courts (outer ring) hear jury trials involving federal issues. Appeals usually go to one of the U.S. Courts of Appeal (middle ring). Among appeals from the latter courts, the U.S. Supreme Court (inner circle) typically hears only those it considers most important.

ORGANIZING SOCIETY

We are in bondage to the law in order that we may be free.
— Cicero, Roman statesman (106–43 B.C.)

Our system of laws is the product of human struggle, through the centuries, to hammer out rules for living together. People have always tended to live in societies—that is, groups such as families, tribes, communities, states.

Societies normally organize to achieve goals that individual members cannot achieve separately. An individual may lack the skill, strength, or time for a certain task. But by division of labor—different individual members doing different things—and by coordinating its efforts, a given group can more likely accomplish the task.

Law is the safest helmet.
— Sir Edward Coke, English jurist (1552–1634)

To help assure that members cooperate in achieving common goals, organized societies have tended to establish **laws,** or rules. These rules help to prevent conflict among a society's members from turning into wasteful violence. Wherever people have lived

TYPICAL STATE COURT SYSTEM

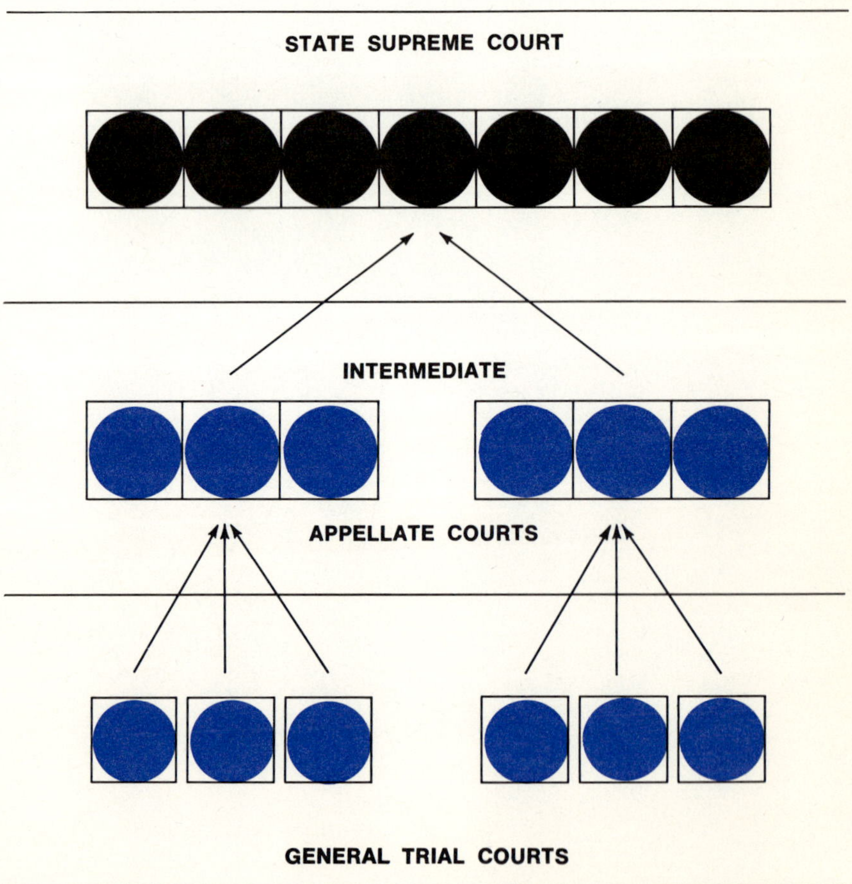

Important civil and criminal cases are tried in general trial courts, usually before a judge and jury. All states have at least one high court, normally called a supreme court, that hears appeals from the general courts. Some states have intermediate courts to lighten the appeals load.

together, some conflict, some clash of interests sooner or later has occurred. Violence, physical injury—even death—often resulted when two members of a society were permitted to settle their own dispute. And the society's wisest and best contributors did not necessarily win these battles. The physically strong usually won. To settle disputes in a peaceable way, the society set up laws. Then, using its collective power, it enforced them.

HERITAGE OF ENGLISH LAW

When they came to America in the seventeenth and eighteenth centuries, English settlers brought with them their home country's system of laws. These laws had evolved over the centuries from trial court decisions in England. The king's judges traveled about the countryside hearing cases that arose in their circuits. Originally, their decisions were based on local customs that varied widely from place to place. Gradually, however, the judges began choosing common legal principles from the decisions and applying them throughout the land. And the system became known as the **common law.**

Under this system, judges based their decisions on **precedents,** or judicial decisions handed down in previous similar cases. This procedure became known as ***stare decisis***—a Latin phrase meaning "to stand by things settled." It enabled courts to provide equal justice. One party in a lawsuit would receive the same treatment as any other in a similar situation. Because judges followed precedents, rather than their own notions of right and wrong, *stare decisis* also insured stable justice. By discovering a legal precedent for a given set of circumstances, citizens could more readily project what their rights and duties would be in that situation.

CONSTITUTIONS AND STATUTES

Principles of the common law were transplanted in the colonial villages and frontier forts of America—primarily through the minds and customs of the English settlers. Law books were scarce. Besides, England's common law was mostly unwritten.

After the American Revolution, the leaders of the United States were determined to clearly define the rights of the people and the rights of their government. Dispute over just such rights, after all, had so recently sparked the guns of revolution. So they put into writing the broadest, most fundamental principles of law that were to govern the nation—in other words, a **constitution.**

Not only the Constitution of the United States, the backbone of our legal system, but also the various state constitutions were written down. Many of the state documents helped the common law take firm root throughout the new nation. They provided that the common law's judicial precedents should govern a given set

If men were angels, no government would be necessary.

— James Madison, 4th President of the United States

Precedents should be overruled when they become inconsistent with present conditions.

— Justice Holmes, *The Common Law* (1881)

of circumstances unless superseded by **statute**—that is, a law written and adopted by a legislature.

Common law rulings were incorporated in constitutions. Statutes—enacted by elected representatives deemed closer than judges to the will of the people—carry out the broad principles of these state constitutions. Constitutional provisions, statutes, and common law precedents all have the force of law. That is, they are enforced by administrative authorities. Statutory law and common law, however, tend to be more specific and limited in scope than constitutional provisions. And statutes, both those enacted by the United States Congress as well as those passed by state legislatures, may change the common law.

The law must be stable, but it must not stand still.

— Roscoe Pound, American jurist (1870–1964)

THRUST OF CONSTANT CHANGE

There is constant change and growth in the American system of law. The law changes whenever a legislature, federal or state, enacts a new statute. Whenever a court interprets such a statute and applies its principles to a concrete set of facts in a lawsuit, the law becomes more specific—and thus changes. Whenever a court stretches an older precedent to fit a new set of facts, the law changes. Whenever a court decides that an older precedent will not stretch far enough to fit a new and entirely different set of circumstances, the court draws a limit on that precedent—and the law changes. Whenever a court finds no earlier precedents as guidelines for a given set of facts, it may establish a trailblazing new precedent. And here, of course, the law changes: boldly, creatively.

The power of precedent, when analyzed, is the power of the beaten track.

— Justice Cardozo, *The Growth of the Law* (1924)

THE SUPREME COURT: CALM IN THE MIDST OF STORMS

Another way of changing the law very special to the American system involves the power to declare laws "unconstitutional." The Constitution, valid laws, and treaties of the United States comprise "the supreme law of the land" (see quote at left). Any conflicting state law or other official act must give way to this "supreme law."

As the nation's highest appellate tribunal, the U.S. Supreme Court is the final interpreter of all federal law. It has the authority to decide whether a law of Congress or an act of the President violates the Constitution. Such a law or act the Court declares **unconstitutional**—that is, illegal and invalid. Likewise, if state laws or acts conflict with the Constitution, they can be set aside.

This Constitution, and the laws of the United States which shall be made in pursuance thereof; and all treaties made, or which shall be made, under the authority of the United States, shall be the supreme law of the land. . . .

— Article VI, Section 2, U.S. Constitution

TRIBUNAL OF FINAL REVIEW

As a tribunal of final review, the Supreme Court established itself, in its infancy, as unique among courts. True, systems of government have always possessed some ultimate determiner of law. Such was a role of the ancient king. Such is the role of the modern dictator. But ironically, never before the establishment of the Supreme Court did this powerful role fall to an independent court of law.

The vast powers of the Supreme Court are shared by the **justices,** or judges. Through history their number has varied. Today there are nine—all appointed for life by a President. In deciding cases, the Chief Justice has but one of nine votes. Chief Justices can, of course, persuade, but in the actual voting they are merely "first among equals." In addition, the Chief Justice presides over sessions and serves as the Court's administrator.

We are under a Constitution but the Constitution is what the judges say it is. . . .

— Chief Justice Hughes, U.S. Supreme Court (1930–1941)

ARGUMENTS AND RECESS

In Washington, D.C., across a tree-flanked street from the great domed Capitol, the Supreme Court conducts its business. Its home is a stately, white marble temple in classical Greek style fronted by Corinthian columns and bearing the inscription: "Equal justice for all."

The Court's term runs from October to June or early July. During that time, the Court follows an alternating schedule. For one two-week period, the justices assemble to hear attorneys argue cases. In the grand courtroom, resplendent in wine-red draperies and marble pillars, the black-robed justices sitting behind a long and imposing mahogany bench face lawyers and spectators. Each party gets roughly an hour to present its case. Justices can and do interrupt counsel with probing questions on law. The exchange is intense. The parry and thrust of keen minds gets as swift as swordplay. Then, in the next two-week period, the justices recess to study the cases and write opinions in their individual chambers or private judicial suites.

BEHIND CLOSED DOORS

On most Fridays during the eight-month term, the justices assemble to confer about the cases. Their seclusion is total. The door of the oak-paneled conference chamber is closed to even the justices' law clerks and secretaries. Beneath a crystal chandelier, flanked by a wall of law books, the nine justices sit around a rectangular table. Here they discuss the cases—freely, sometimes heatedly, without fear that their remarks may be reported in the press and perhaps misinterpreted by the public.

The Chief Justice of the United States opens the discussion on every case. The Chief Justice's role is to summarize the facts, state the issues of law, and give suggestions on how to solve them. Then the Chief Justice calls on each of the associate justices—from the most senior justice to the most junior—to present his or her views.

Opinions are required in our legal system in order that the reasoning which justifies a conclusion may be made manifest.

— Justice Frankfurter, *Darr v. Burford* (1950)

SPLIT DECISION

A majority vote decides the **ruling,** or the Court's conclusion of law as to the legal effect of the facts in any given case. When all justices vote, and they normally do, a majority requires at least a 5 to 4 vote. For a quorum there must be at least six justices voting, in which case a majority of 4 to 2 would be required. The vote, of course, may be unanimous. But with nine strong-minded justices, "split decisions" are common. The **majority opinion** represents the Court's official statement of the case, giving its ruling and expounding the reasoning behind it.

> Even this Court has the last say only for a time. Being composed of fallible men, it may err. But revision of its errors must be by orderly process of law.
>
> — Justice Frankfurter, *United States v. United Mine Workers* (1947)

When a justice agrees with the decision, or ruling, of the majority, but disagrees with its reasoning, he or she may write a **concurring opinion.** A justice who disagrees with the majority's decision may write a **dissenting opinion.** Although dissents do not represent an official precedent, the wisely reasoned ones often influence the thinking of justices in later decisions. The Court can, and sometimes does, overrule itself. The only other way to set aside, or **nullify,** a Supreme Court decision is by the lengthy process of amending the Constitution.

VITAL ISSUES ONLY

In a given year, courts in modern America may try 10 million cases, but only a tiny fraction ever achieve a complete airing in the U.S. Supreme Court. Fewer than 5,000 applications for review are made to the Supreme Court. And of these, the high bench may agree to rule on perhaps 200. Even then, the Court disposes of many cases by ***per curiam opinions***—that is, brief and unsigned rulings that do not spell out the legal reasoning behind them.

The overwhelming majority of applications for review, then, are rejected by the Court—on grounds (1) that it agrees with the holding of the lower court, or (2) that the case contains no "substantial federal question." To begin with, the Court's legal **jurisdiction,** or the authority to hear and render judgment, is limited to federal questions. These involve the interpretation and application of the Constitution, acts of Congress, and treaties. By itself, this limitation removes from review by the Supreme Court the vast majority of American law cases. These involve state laws, laws governing such matters as property sales, theft, and burglary. To insure that it has time for full, careful deliberation of the most vital constitutional issues, the Court even further restricts itself to "substantial" federal questions.

NATIONAL POLICYMAKER

Over the years, the Constitution and the Congress have left the Court almost complete discretion in selecting the cases it reviews. Increasingly, the Court has allowed lower appellate courts to reach the final decision in most cases. Being free to concentrate on the big questions, the really vital issues of the Constitution, has enabled the Supreme Court to play a key role in making national policy.

BILL OF RIGHTS

The Constitution that was drawn up by delegates to the Constitutional Convention in 1787 did not contain a "bill of rights." This was the most serious criticism levelled against the Constitution in the conventions later ratifying, or formally approving, the document. What a number of states wanted was a series of amendments that would protect fundamental individual rights against interference by the federal government. Several states ratified with the condition that a bill of rights be added.

When the first Congress of the United States met in 1789, representatives drafted the Bill of Rights, or first ten amendments to the Constitution. These were quickly ratified by the states and became part of the Constitution in 1791.

The Bill of Rights was intended to protect individuals from actions of the federal government. These amendments did not originally apply to the states. In 1868, the Fourteenth Amendment was added to the Constitution. A part of that amendment provides that no state shall "deprive any person of life, liberty or property, without due process of law." By the 1890's, the United States Supreme Court had ruled that the **due process clause** prohibits the states from restricting the exercise of property rights in a number of ways.

No state shall make or enforce any law which shall abridge the privileges or immunities of citizens of the United States; nor shall any state deprive any person of life, liberty, or property, without due process of law; nor deny to any person within its jurisdiction the equal protection of the laws.

— 14th Amendment, U.S. Constitution (1868)

In the twentieth century, the Court has dramatically enlarged the liberties of the individual. Since the 1920's the Court has held—in a series of separate cases—that the Fourteenth Amendment (see quote at left) also protects many liberties listed in the Bill of Rights against encroachment by the states. These have long been fundamental rights in our national code of values: the liberties of free speech, press, and religion (First Amendment); the guarantees against unreasonable searches and seizures (Fourth Amendment); and, in criminal prosecutions, the right of accused persons to remain silent (Fifth Amendment), to get help from an attorney (Sixth Amendment), to confront the witnesses against them (Sixth Amendment), and to be secure from cruel and unusual punishments (Eighth Amendment).

RIGHTS IN CONFLICT

The Supreme Court cases in this book dig into each of these pivotal areas. Yet the scope of this book is larger than just the "Bill of Rights." Indeed, landmark cases in the following chapters cover the great unsettled issues of American society. You will examine these issues in epochs of history when they became important. And you will trace their evolution down to present times.

The ultimate function of the Supreme Court is nothing less than the arbitration between fundamental and ever-present rival forces. . . in our organized society.

— Justice Jackson, *Struggle for Judicial Supremacy* (1941)

Not only are these cases significant. They also thunder with the drama of our often stormy history. Together, they unfold a narrative of rights in conflict. Your guide along this pilgrimage will be the Supreme Court: tribunal of final review, maker of national policy.

1 Freedom of Belief

The three prisoners marched under guard through the streets of colonial Boston. They tried to call out to clusters of people along the way. But Puritan officials had the three surrounded by drummers who drowned their words. When they stepped onto the Boston Common, the October afternoon sun was slanting down on the great elm tree: the hanging elm. The prisoners walked hand in hand now, William Robinson and Marmaduke Stevenson on the outside, Mary Dyer in the middle. As they approached the scaffold, the huge crowd rustled with tension.

Many were uncomfortable that the three had been condemned simply because they were Quakers.

These Quakers had challenged the wrath of the Puritan clergy. And here, in Massachusetts Bay Colony during 1659, the Puritans were a powerful force—and as severe as the rockbound coast. The colony's official church was the Congregationalist or Puritan. Its congregations formed the fundamental social units in the villages; its chosen ministers were the foremost leaders. Only "visible saints" who had led blameless lives could become church members. Only church members could vote in town elections. The Bible served as a strict guide for life's problems, civil as well as religious. It contained the will of God, and that will was interpreted by the Puritan clergy. Their interpretations became civic law—not because the ministers held public office, but because of their great influence over government officials. The clergy felt that their theocracy, a union of church and state, was vital to the colony's survival.

Other churches were not welcome. Especially Quakers. These crusading nonconformists would not pay tithes, take oaths, or bear arms. Preaching the equality of all men and women, they refused to take off their hats in the presence of "superiors." Even more alarming to the Puritan clergy was the Quaker belief that God communicated directly with every person. This doctrine of "inward light" posed a threat to the dominant power of the Puritan ministry: it implied that ministers were unnecessary.

To rid the Holy Commonwealth of this threat, Puritan elders waged a relentless campaign. Quakers were imprisoned, whipped, branded, and starved. Some had their ears cut off. When these measures failed, the elders urged one still harsher. Their proposed bill before the General Court, or legislature, would banish—under pain of death—any known Quaker.

At first, members of the court resisted the bill. Many felt it too radical. But according to one colonial source, "the priests and the rulers were all for blood, and they pursued it." In October of 1658, the measure finally passed, 13 to 12.

A year later, William Robinson and Marmaduke Stevenson and Mary Dyer became the first Quakers to be condemned under the controversial statute. All three Quaker missionaries previously had been banished from Massachusetts Bay; then they had returned precisely to "look the bloody Puritan law in the face."

Robinson was the first to die. Next came Stevenson. Then Mary Dyer climbed the scaffold. The hangman placed the blindfold over her eyes, the rope around her neck.

"Stop!" shouted a voice in the crowd. "She is reprieved!" Officials rushed forward and took her down.

The General Court had planned this tactic when they sentenced Mary Dyer to die. They hoped to regain the favor of the crowd as well as to frighten her from challenging the anti-Quaker law again.

Illustration Analysis

Analyze the pictures on pages 12–13. How do you think the photograph of students in a public school classroom is related to the photo of the church? What message, if any, about freedom of religion does this design communicate by juxtaposing these two photographs? How does the silhouetted wall of a church relate to constitutional problems over "establishment of religion"? What does the row of helmets upon rifles symbolize? How do you think this motif relates to "freedom of belief"? What message, if any, do you think this design communicates by rendering the illustration of the Quaker, Mary Dyer, partly in black-on-white and partly in white-on-black?

Once more Mary Dyer was banished from Massachusetts Bay. A half-year later, she returned. This time she was marched to the gallows, once more to the rumble of drums, and straightaway hanged.

IN YOUR OPINION

1. In your own words, what behavior did the Quaker banishment law punish? Do you think that a government should have the right to control such behavior? Why? Do you think that the types of punishment used by the Puritans to control such behavior were justified? Why?
2. How free should citizens of the United States be today to hold whatever religious beliefs and to worship in whatever way they choose? What restrictions, if any, should the government make on religious beliefs and worship? Explain your answers.
3. How great a threat to the welfare of the Massachusetts Bay Colony do you think was posed by the Quaker beliefs and practices?
4. How necessary do you think a theocracy was to Massachusetts Bay Colony's survival in a harsh environment? What strengths stemmed from the union of church and state? What problems and dangers stemmed from such a policy?
5. In modern American society, to what extent, if any, should church and state be unified? Explain.
6. What part of the Constitution deals with the freedom of religious belief and practice, and with the separation of church and state?

FOUNTAINHEAD OF TOLERANCE

Religion, or the duty which we owe to our Creator, and the manner of discharging it, can be directed only by reason and conviction, not by force or violence; and therefore all men are equally entitled to the free exercise of religion, according to the dictates of conscience; and . . . it is the mutual duty of all to practise Christian forebearance, love, and charity towards each other.

— The Virginia Bill of Rights (1776)

"It hath been found by experience," said a 1704 statute in South Carolina establishing the Church of England as the official church for the colony, "that the admitting of persons of different persuasions and interest in matters of religion . . . hath often caused great contentions and animosities in this Province, and hath very much obstructed the public business. . . ."

The reasoning offered in this law prevailed in most of the early colonies. Many of the Europeans who settled America were religious dissenters. At home, in England or on the European mainland, they had frequently been forced to join the "established," or official, church—or at least support it by paying taxes collected by the government. When they arrived in North America, these groups were determined in their own colonies to secure religious freedom for themselves. They were often less interested in guaranteeing this liberty for others. As a result, they set up their own established churches.

In New England colonies, the Congregational Church often became the official one. In Southern colonies, the Anglican Church was usually established. Intolerance toward other sects took several forms. Like Massachusetts Bay, Virginia expelled Quakers. New Jersey prevented them from voting. North Carolina and New Hampshire limited the vote to Protestants. Maryland, founded mainly as a haven for Catholics, tolerated most other Christian sects but banned Unitarians and Jews. Even Pennsylvania, settled as a sanctuary for the widely persecuted Quakers, limited freedom of worship to Christians.

THE REVOLUTION

The common cause of the American Revolution (1775–1783) lessened religious intolerance. The political power of the clergy waned. Seeds of our constitutional principles of religious freedom were being planted—especially in the fertile soil of Virginia. In 1776, the important "Virginia Bill of Rights" was adopted. Included in it was a section, drafted by the great patriot, Patrick Henry, outlining "the free exercise of religion" (see quote, page 15). Not until a decade later, however, and only after a long and bitter struggle, did Virginia's General Assembly pass Thomas Jefferson's "Statute of Religious Liberty" (see quote at left). The effect of that document was to deprive the Anglican Church of official support.

Be it enacted by the General Assembly, that no man shall be compelled to frequent or support any religious worship, place or ministry whatsoever, nor shall be enforced, restrained, molested, or burthened in his body or goods, nor shall otherwise suffer on account of his religious opinions or belief; but that all men shall be free to profess, and by argument to maintain, their opinion in matters of religion, and that the same shall in no wise diminish, enlarge or affect their civil capacities.

— Thomas Jefferson, Virginia Statute of Religious Liberty (1786)

When the Constitution and Bill of Rights were adopted, Americans could hardly have agreed on a single church. There was too great a diversity of religions in the Thirteen States. Indeed, five states still had official churches. It was only natural, therefore, that the First Amendment (see quote, center left) provided in part that "Congress shall make no law respecting an establishment of religion."

ESTABLISHMENT CLAUSE

Congress shall make no law respecting an establishment of religion, or prohibiting the free exercise thereof. . . .

— 1st Amendment, U.S. Constitution (1791)

Although this **establishment clause** prohibited the setting up of a national church, it did not apply—at the time—to official churches existing in the states. Later, these states themselves withdrew support from their churches. (And still later, the U.S. Supreme Court ruled that, under the Fourteenth Amendment, all clauses of the First Amendment applied to state governments as well as to the federal.)

Beyond the ban on a national church, constitutional experts have sharply disagreed ever since about the meaning of the establishment clause. Some claim that it merely kept the government from favoring one sect over another. Others urge a far broader interpretation. They point to James Madison, who proposed the first ten amendments. He opposed any relationship between church and state, no matter how slight. They also cite Thomas Jefferson. In his 1802 letter to the Danbury Baptists, Jefferson said that he believed the First Amendment was designed to erect "a wall of separation between church and state" (see quote at left).

I contemplate with solemn reverence that act of the whole American people which declared that their legislature should "make no law respecting an establishment of religion, or prohibiting the free exercise thereof," thus building a wall of separation between church and state,

— President Thomas Jefferson, Letter to the Danbury Baptist Association (1802)

FREE EXERCISE CLAUSE

Such a differing of interpretations never developed over the First Amendment's **free exercise clause.** Basically, it has been held to protect a citizen's freedom (1) of religious beliefs and (2) of activities that flow naturally from those beliefs. Although beliefs have been fully protected, the activities have been restricted at times—particularly when they interfered with more important rights of society.

The cases in this and every chapter progress in chronological order. They indicate how the Supreme Court has come to grips with vital issues down through time. As you analyze the cases in this chapter, try to decide which involve "establishment" problems and which, "free exercise" problems.

REYNOLDS V. UNITED STATES (1879)

Because of their beliefs, the Mormons encountered hostility from other Christians. Under the strong authority of their founder and prophet, Joseph Smith, they became a theocracy in search of a home. First they settled in Ohio, then Missouri, then Illinois. Here, in 1844, Smith was murdered. The incident triggered a two-year reign of violence across the countryside. Then Brigham Young, who had succeeded Smith, led thousands of his people on a long trek westward to their "promised land," the harsh and arid flats around the Great Salt Lake in Utah. By large-scale irrigation projects tapping mountain-slope streams, the pioneer colony grew and prospered. Then the United States, which had acquired Utah in a treaty with Mexico, organized it into a territory in 1850. All too soon, one of the practices approved by the Mormon Church came into conflict with American law.

George Reynolds had two wives. Both of them were living. He was a leading official of the Mormon Church; and like other Mormons in the Utah Territory in 1874, he believed in polygamy, or plural marriages.

In 1847, when the Mormons first settled in Utah, they were free to practice their religion as they believed. Once non-Mormons began to settle in the territory, however, Congress began getting demands for legislation to end the "immoral practice" of plural marriages. Polygamy, opponents said, traditionally had been a serious crime throughout the Western world. It had generally been considered an offense against society, except in Asia and Africa.

In 1862 Congress passed the Anti-Bigamy Act, which read: "Every person having a husband or wife living, who married another, whether married or single, in a territory, or other place over which the United States have exclusive jurisdiction, is guilty of bigamy, and shall be punished by a fine of not more than $500, and by imprisonment for a term of not more than five years."

After the Civil War (1861–1865), this act was used in a relentless drive to wipe out the Mormon practice of plural marriages. George Reynolds was one of many members of the Mormon Church to be arrested and tried under the statute in the 1870's.

At his trial, Reynolds claimed that he had suffered severe migraine headaches from the anxiety of trying to make "plural marriages successful in a hostile environment." He argued that one of the doctrines of his church required male members to practice polygamy whenever they could. (The founder, Joseph Smith, who instituted the practice after he said he had experienced a vision suggesting it, left 27 widows when he died.) Mormons who did not practice polygamy would suffer "damnation in the life to come."

Reynolds felt strongly that the law against polygamy was wrong. He asked the trial court to instruct the jury to bring in a verdict of not guilty if the evidence indicated that he had taken a second wife as a religious duty. The court refused. Instead, the judge charged that if the defendant had married a second time, with a first wife living, his religious beliefs did not justify his breaking a law of the land. Under such circumstances, added the judge, the defendant would have knowingly violated a law—and it would not matter whether his intent was criminal or religious.

The jury found Reynolds guilty. He was sentenced to two years in prison and fined $500. Reynolds appealed his case to the Supreme Court of the United States, claiming that the 1862 Anti-Bigamy Act interfered with his freedom of religion.

FOR CRITICAL THINKING

1. Would you classify this case as an "establishment of religion" or a "free exercise" problem? Explain.
2. Why did Reynolds feel that he should not be convicted of having committed a crime—even though he had broken the law? Explain your answer.
3. What did Reynolds think would be the consequences to him if he did not practice polygamy?
4. What reasons do you think society might have for banning polygamy? Do you think these reasons justify a law against plural marriage? Explain your answers.
5. Does the quotation from Chief Justice Waite (at left) help you decide this case? Explain. Do you think it is from a majority or a dissenting opinion? Why? Do you agree with Waite's ideas about marriage? Explain.
6. How do you think the Supreme Court ruled in this case?

> Marriage, while from its . . . nature a sacred obligation, is nevertheless, in most civilized nations, a civil contract, and usually regulated by law. Upon it society may be said to be built, and out of its fruits spring social relations and social obligations and duties with which government is necessarily required to deal.
>
> — Chief Justice Waite, *Reynolds v. U.S.* (1879)

EVERSON V. BOARD OF EDUCATION (1947)

A touchy area of controversy in freedom of religion has been that of public education and its relationship to private religious schools. When the First Amendment was adopted, education was not widely supported by public funds. Not until the mid-nineteenth century did the movement to provide free, tax-supported elementary and secondary schools gather momentum. As immigration mushroomed in the 1800's, the number of private, church-affiliated schools grew—especially Roman Catholic schools. In Pierce v. Society of Sisters *(1925), the U.S. Supreme Court ruled that parents have the right to fulfill the compulsory education laws by sending their children to private religious schools—as long as these were accredited, or approved by the state. Then, still another constitutional problem came up in the following case.*

Arch Everson, a New Jersey taxpayer, was angry. He strongly objected to state funds being used to pay bus fares of children going to Catholic schools. He filed a lawsuit against his school board to stop this aid, being distributed under a state law.

According to the New Jersey law, district boards of education could contract for the transportation of children who lived "remote from any schoolhouse." The township of Ewing, New Jersey, did not have a public high school. So township teenagers took the local bus to high school in neighboring Trenton or Pennington. Some Catholic children from Ewing also took the local bus to Trenton to attend parochial schools—both elementary and high school. Ewing's board of education reimbursed parents for the bus fares paid by Catholic as well as public school students.

In his lawsuit, Everson maintained that the statute violated his right to freedom of religion. The New Jersey court agreed with Everson. It held that when citizens are forced to pay taxes to help support religious schools, this is the same as state aid to religion. And that, said the court, is prohibited by the First Amendment, as applied to the states by the Fourteenth Amendment.

New Jersey's highest court, which heard the case next, reversed the decision. In doing so, it stated that the tax funds were being used for a public service—the transportation directly benefited parents and children. The funds, added the state high court, were not a contribution to the schools as institutions. The court also said that the state made attendance at an accredited school compulsory, and the transportation statute helped carry out the attendance statute.

The "establishment of religion" clause . . . means at least this: Neither a state nor the federal government can set up a church. Neither can pass laws which aid one religion, aid all religions, or prefer one religion over another. Neither can force nor influence a person to go or to remain away from church against his will or force him to profess a belief or disbelief in any religion. No person can be punished for entertaining or professing religious beliefs or disbeliefs, for church attendance or non-attendance. No tax in any amount, large or small, can be levied to support any religious activities or institutions. . . .

— Justice Black, *Everson v. Board of Education* (1947)

FOR CRITICAL THINKING

1. Would you classify this problem as an "establishment of religion" case or a "free exercise" problem? Why?
2. Reread the ruling of *Pierce v. Society of Sisters* (1925) in the headnote of this case. If under that ruling children can go to either public or religious schools to fulfill state school attendance requirements, do you think both types of schools should receive equal public funding? Why or why not?
3. If a town does not have public school facilities, should it have the power to provide bus fares so its students can attend school

Here parents pay money to send their children to parochial schools and funds raised by taxation are used to reimburse them. This not only helps the children to get to school and the parents to send them. It aids them in a substantial way to get the very thing which they are sent to the particular school to secure, namely, religious training and teaching. . . .

— Justice Rutledge, *Everson v. Board of Education* (1947)

elsewhere? If yes, should it provide bus fares to only public schools? To public and nonreligious private schools? To any nonprofit schools? To any schools? Explain your answers.

4. If the state pays for transporting children to parochial school, should it also pay for teachers' salaries and textbooks at the parochial school? Why or why not? If yes, should the state pay the expenses for all courses at the parochial school—or only some courses? If only some courses, what type of courses?

5. Does the quote from Justice Black (page 19) help you decide this case? Explain. Does the quote from Justice Rutledge (left) help you? Explain. Which, if either, do you think is from a majority opinion? A concurring opinion? A dissenting opinion? Explain.

6. How do you think the Supreme Court ruled in this case?

ABINGTON SCHOOL DISTRICT V. SCHEMPP (1963)

To what extent should religious practices be allowed in public schools? In the early 1960's, this issue reached the boiling point. First there was Engel v. Vitale *(1962). Here, the New York State Board of Regents had composed a short, nondenominational prayer for recitation by students. The U.S. Supreme Court ruled that the exercise violated the First Amendment. The state could not "prescribe by law any particular prayer which is to be used as an official prayer in carrying on any program of governmentally sponsored religious activity."*

The decision stirred passionate debate across the country. Part of the reason was the concurring opinion of Justice William O. Douglas. He urged the outlawing of any trace of religion from official public life—including the use of chaplains by government, devotional statements by a President, or tax concessions for religious institutions. The next year, the Supreme Court faced an equally stormy issue in the following case.

As their classmates stood and recited the Lord's Prayer to begin the school day, Roger and Donna Schempp fumed. They tried to close their ears when the intercom system boomed Bible verses into their classroom at Abington Senior High.

Roger and Donna and their parents, because of their personal religious beliefs, objected to these exercises that took place daily in the Abington, Pennsylvania, public schools. The family filed a lawsuit in a federal district court to stop the Abington School District from conducting the prayers and readings, which were required by state law. The Pennsylvania statute stated: "At least ten verses from the Holy Bible shall be read, without comment, at the opening of each public school on each school day. Any child shall be excused from such Bible reading, or attending such Bible reading, upon the written request of his parent or guardian." The Schempps argued that this law violated their constitutional rights under the First Amendment.

At the trial, the Schempps claimed that the classroom exercises involved a literal reading of the Bible. And this, they said, conveyed doctrines that were contrary to their deeply held religious beliefs.

Mr. Schempp testified that he had decided not to have his children excused from the exercises, even though the law allowed it. He contended that this would have hurt their relationships with their teachers and classmates. If Roger and Donna had been excused, they would have to stand in the hallway outside the classroom. They would have felt like "oddballs" or looked as though they were being punished.

The school district argued that the Bible—because of its great literary, historical, and moral value—was an important part of any educational program. It offered non-religious values useful to society. Besides, unless the schools provided some religious exercises, they would seem to foster a "religion of secularism" and actually be hostile toward religion. The school district added that Americans have historically been a religious people. It cited recent figures indicating that 64 percent of U.S. citizens belonged to a church, while only 3 percent claimed no religion at all.

A federal district court held that the Pennsylvania statute requiring Bible reading in the public schools violated the First Amendment, as applied to the states by the Fourteenth Amendment. The court said this was true in spite of the provision for excusing a student from the reading. The Abington School District appealed to the U.S. Supreme Court.

While the free exercise clause clearly prohibits the use of state action to deny the rights of free exercise to anyone, it has never meant that a majority could use the machinery of the state to practice its beliefs.

— Justice Clark, *Abington School District v. Schempp* (1963)

FOR CRITICAL THINKING

1. Would you classify this case as an "establishment of religion" case or a "free exercise" case? Why?
2. Do you think the use of the Bible in the opening exercises was more in the nature of an educational program or of a religious service? Explain your answer.
3. How do you think students excused from the exercises would feel as they stood outside the classroom during opening exercises? How, if in any way, should the potential feelings of such students have influenced those who enacted the law?
4. If a public school does not hold any religious exercises, does this indicate a particular attitude or position about religion? Explain.
5. If a majority of citizens wanted Bible readings in schools, should the state legislature let a minority opposed to it block the passage of a law requiring such exercises? Why or why not?
6. Does the First Amendment say a person is free to have no religion? Do you think the First Amendment applies equally to people holding religious beliefs and to those who profess no religious beliefs? Explain your answer.
7. Does the quotation from Justice Clark (above) help you decide this case? Explain. Does the quotation from Justice Stewart (at left) help you? Explain. Which, if either, do you think is from a majority opinion? A concurring opinion? A dissenting opinion?
8. How do you think the Supreme Court ruled in this case?

A compulsory state educational system so [forms] a child's life that if religious exercises are to be a [banned] activity in schools, religion is placed at an artificial . . . disadvantage. . . . And a refusal to permit religious exercises thus is seen, not as . . . state neutrality, but rather as the establishment of a religion of secularism. . . .

— Justice Stewart, *Abington School District v. Schempp* (1963)

WELSH V. UNITED STATES (1970)

Drafting men for war has historically provoked controversy in America. In the Civil War (1861–1865), conscription led to draft riots in the North. One riot left as many as 1,200 persons dead in New York City. Much of the opposition to a draft has been based on religious convictions, and federal law has at least recognized these. The Union's draft statute, for instance, exempted from military service persons forbidden by their church doctrines to bear arms. Typical were members of the Quaker, Mennonite, and Amish faiths.

To characterize the views of such persons, the term "conscientious objector" came into use in World War I (1914–1918). During World War II (1939–1945), Congress allowed a broader exemption. Opposition to war could now be based on "religious training and belief." This phrase was expanded considerably by the Supreme Court during the Vietnam conflict—the longest war in U.S. history and an unpopular one. In United States v. Seeger *(1965), the Court said that objectors need not believe in a Supreme Being. But "sincere and meaningful belief" must nevertheless occupy the same place in their lives as an orthodox religious belief might occupy in the lives of other persons. Then, in the following case, an objector asked the Court to stretch the interpretation still further.*

To Elliott Welsh, a young computer engineer from Los Angeles, killing in war was unethical and immoral. In 1964, as America's involvement in Vietnam grew, he applied to his local draft board to be classified as a "conscientious objector"—thus beginning a series of legal obstacles and defeats, including a prison sentence, that would eventually carry him before the highest court in the land.

According to the Universal Military Training and Service Act, a person could be exempted from both combat and noncombat military service who, "by reason of religious training and belief, is conscientiously opposed to participation in war in any form." The phrase "religious training and belief" meant belief in a Supreme Being but did not include "essentially political, sociological, or philosophical views or a merely personal moral code."

Although Welsh grew up in a religious family, the church he attended did not teach its members that taking part in war was evil. When he first registered for the draft, in 1961, he did not claim to be a "C.O." It was not until three years later that he applied for the exemption. At that time, Welsh belonged to no church. He said that his pacifist beliefs had been formed "by reading in the fields of history and sociology." On his exemption application, he declared that he could neither affirm nor deny belief in a Supreme Being. And, before signing the statement, "I am, by reason of my religious training and belief, conscientiously opposed to participation in war in any form," Welsh crossed out the words *religious training and.*

In a letter to his draft board, Welsh wrote: "I can only act according to what I am and what I see. And I see that the military complex wastes both human and material resources, that it fosters disregard for (what I consider a paramount concern) human needs and ends; I see the means we employ to 'defend' our 'way of life' profoundly change that way of life. . . ."

Welsh also made a statement that he believed the taking of life "to be morally wrong."

His local draft board turned down his application. Welsh appealed to an appeal board in the Selective Service System, but it concluded that his beliefs were not sufficiently "religious" to meet the terms of the draft law. When he refused to submit to induction, Welsh was arrested. A federal district court tried, convicted, and sentenced him to three years in prison. Welsh appealed his conviction to a U.S. Court of Appeals. This tribunal noted that Welsh held his beliefs as strongly as more traditional, church-affiliated "C.O.'s." But the court said that since Welsh himself had declared his beliefs to be based on sociology and history rather than religion, the Selective Service System was entitled to deny his request for "C.O." classification.

Welsh brought his case to the U.S. Supreme Court, contending that the draft law violated his First Amendment right.

FOR CRITICAL THINKING

1. Would you classify this case as an "establishment of religion" problem or a "free exercise" problem? Explain.
2. How do you interpret the meaning of the words "religious training and belief" as they are used in the federal draft law?
3. How do you think Welsh changed the application by crossing out the words *religious training and?*
4. Interpret in your own words what Welsh meant by his letter.
5. From his letter, his statements, and his "C.O." application with the crossed-out words, what was the basis of Welsh's objection to the draft?
6. Do you agree or disagree with the U.S. Court of Appeals that the Selective Service System should be entitled to take Welsh at his word when he denied that his objection to war was based on religious beliefs? Explain.
7. How do you think the Supreme Court ruled in this case?

WALLACE V. JAFFREE (1985)

Among the most controversial constitutional issues are those involving religion and the schools. In a number of Supreme Court decisions in the early 1960's, school prayer and Bible readings were declared unconstitutional. The Court emphasized that government must be neutral—that it must neither support nor oppose religion.

In time, many state legislatures, concerned that school children were being denied a chance to share in the nation's spiritual heritage, sought ways around those rulings. About half the states enacted laws that allowed teachers to hold "moments of silence." How, though, was a "moment of silence" to be used? The following case dealt with that sensitive issue.

Ishmael Jaffree began his life as a child evangelist on the street corners of Cleveland, urging sinners to get right with God. Little did he know that as an adult he would take the state of Alabama to court over the issue of school prayer.

It all started in 1982 when Jaffree, now a lawyer in Mobile, asked his five-year-old son what he was learning in school. To his surprise, the boy started to repeat a prayer often recited in the class by his teacher.

Jaffree, who over the years had lost his faith and become an agnostic, was stunned. He thought Alabama was destroying the constitutional separation of church and state. He also thought Alabama was undermining his efforts to raise his children as "free thinkers."

Until 1981 the state legislature had mandated that Alabama schools start the day with a moment of silence "for meditation." But in that year the legislature added the words "or voluntary prayer" to the law. The legislature also permitted teachers to lead students in a vocal prayer to God as "the Creator and Supreme Judge of the World."

Jaffree went to court to challenge the 1981 law. By so doing, he caused an uproar. Alabama Governor Fob James called a special session of the state legislature to pass a bill authorizing prayer in the public schools. Included in the bill was a prayer written by the governor's son. Jaffree also faced public anger. Schoolmates harrassed his children, and the family started getting nasty letters, threatening phone calls, and eggs thrown at their house.

Jaffree pressed on, demanding that Alabama's moment-of-silence law be struck down. He said that the legislature's only purpose had been to promote religious activity in the classroom. He cited the testimony of the law's chief sponsor in the Alabama Senate. When asked whether his legislation had any goal other than prayer in the schools, Senator Donald Holmes answered, "No, I [had] no other purpose in mind."

Alabama made no effort to defend the law beyond saying that the legislature wanted "to return voluntary prayer to the schools." In its first court test the law was upheld. Federal District Judge W. Brevard Hand ruled that the Supreme Court's views to the contrary, the Constitution did not prevent the states from establishing an official religion. The U.S. Court of Appeals quickly overturned Hand's decision. The case then went before the Supreme Court.

FOR CRITICAL THINKING

1. Would you classify this case as an "establishment of religion" case, or a "free exercise" case? Why?

2. What objection did Ishmael Jaffree have to the 1981 Alabama law? How did the state of Alabama counter his argument?
3. Do you agree that a school prayer would have interfered with Jaffree's efforts to raise his children as "free thinkers"? Why or why not?
4. Do you think a law requiring prayer in school is unconstitutional? What about a law requiring meditation? What is the difference?
5. How do you think the Supreme Court ruled in this case?

EXPLORING THE MAIN IDEAS

WHAT DO YOU THINK?

1. Do you agree with Justice Black's majority opinion or Justice Rutledge's dissenting opinion in the *Everson* case? Why?
2. After rereading this chapter's background note on "Fountainhead of Tolerance," as well as any cases that deal with "establishment of religion," which interpretation of the establishment clause do you support: (a) the complete "wall of separation" theory, or (b) the less sweeping one restricting government from favoring one religion over another? Give reasons for your position.
3. Do you agree or disagree with the rule in the *Reynolds* case upholding the law against polygamy as constitutional? Do you think marriage is an area of social and moral life appropriately controlled by the government? Do you think a law against unmarried people living together would be constitutional? Explain your answers.

Illustration Review

Now that you have finished this chapter's cases, re-analyze the pictures on pages 12–13. Which cases relate to which pictures? In what ways, if any, would your answers to the questions in "Illustration Analysis" at the beginning of the chapter now change? In what ways, if any, would your answers remain the same?

THINGS TO DO

1. Assume that you are attorney for your local school board. In a short written report, advise the board whether you think there is any constitutional way for elementary teachers to treat the Old Testament story of Joseph and his brothers in a public school classroom. Also offer advice about the New Testament story of the Good Samaritan. Support your arguments with Supreme Court reasoning from this chapter.
2. Read Arthur Miller's powerful play, *The Crucible.* Discuss in class the issues of church and state, as well as freedom of conscience, raised by the playwright. In the light of our constitutional principles today, how would you have solved those issues in 1692 at Salem?
3. Using procedures outlined in the back of this book, put on a mock trial of the *Welsh* case.

The

2 Freedom of Expression

The colonial chief justice sat sweating in his red velvet robe and long white wig. As the jury was picked, the heat was stifling this August day in 1735. And tension among the spectators turned the jam-packed courtroom in New York into a steam oven. For this was the showdown in a conflict between the royal governor and a newspaper editor: the trial of John Peter Zenger.

Zenger's *New York Weekly Journal* had been founded by members of the colony's rising merchant class. Its role was to oppose policies of the new governor, William Cosby, and his supporters among the class of old, wealthy families. And from its very first edition, in 1733, the *Journal* did just that. It accused Cosby of rigging elections to put his favorites in office. It claimed that he allowed French ships to spy on the British colonial defenses in the bay. And it ridiculed the governor's officials as incompetent. The spicy sheet was eagerly read in the Black Horse and other taverns all over town.

Cosby was furious. No American newspaper had ever dared challenge the government so boldly. He tried to get a grand jury to indict Zenger. It refused. Finally, after much legal maneuvering, the governor arranged for his attorney general, Richard Bradley, to file an information. Arrested and jailed, Zenger faced a charge of "seditious libel"—that is, criticising the government in a manner threatening its security.

As the trial opened, Bradley thought he could scent an easy victory. The chief justice, James De Lancey, was hand-picked by Governor Cosby. And though Zenger's younger attorney entered a plea of "not guilty," his opening statement lacked fire and sureness. Then, suddenly, in the back of the courtroom, an elegant old man with white hair tumbling to his shoulders stood and introduced himself as Andrew Hamilton. The room hushed. Heads craned for a look. *Andrew Hamilton* of Philadelphia, the most famous lawyer in all the colonies! He'd been secretly hired by Zenger's supporters.

"I cannot think it proper for me," Hamilton began, "to deny the publication of a complaint, which I think is the right of every freeborn subject to make, when the matters so published can be supported with truth." Dramatically, he then admitted that his client had published the critical articles. Zenger's friends gasped. The governor's supporters were overjoyed. Both figured the old lawyer had just thrown the editor's case away. Bradley cockily said there was nothing left to do but for the jury to return a verdict of "guilty."

Illustration Analysis

Analyze the pictures on pages 26–27. What message, if any, does this routing of eye movement communicate about the interrelation of the press, news events, and the citizen? What means of expression are involved in this design? Which elements are advancing freedom of expression? Which elements are limiting freedom of expression?

Hamilton, however, argued that the *Journal's* accusations were true—and that truth was a good defense to the charge. A libel, he said, is a *false* statement that injures the victim's reputation. When Chief Justice De Lancey interrupted to disagree, Hamilton coolly bowed and turned to the jury. "Then it is to you gentlemen," said the Philadelphian. "We must now appeal for witnesses to the truth of the facts we have offered."

De Lancey cut in again. The jury could decide whether Zenger published the articles. But only judges may decide whether the articles were libelous.

"The jury may do so," Hamilton fired back. "But I do likewise know they may do otherwise."

For the rest of the trial, Hamilton practically ignored the judges' bench. He addressed the jury directly, intently, urging them to follow their free consciences. In his ringing summation, Hamilton declared that "the question before the court and you gentlemen of the jury is not of small nor private concern. . . . No! It may in its consequence affect every free man that lives under a British government on the main of America. It is the best cause. It is the cause of liberty."

IN YOUR OPINION

1. How do you think the colonial jury decided in the Zenger trial? How do you think the jury should have decided? Explain your answer.
2. Do you think our Constitution should protect as "free speech" any published lies that injure a person's reputation? Explain.
3. To what extent, if any, do you think the Constitution should protect as "free speech" any published references to sex and sexual morality? Explain your answer.
4. To what extent, if any, do you think the Constitution ought to protect as "free speech" any criticism of our government?
5. What limitations, if any, do you think the Constitution should place on a citizen's right of free speech? What part or parts of the Constitution do you think are involved with such rights?

BOUNDARIES OF EXPRESSION

The march of Western history had brought John Peter Zenger into the courtroom that hot August day in 1735. Since the earliest European use of the printing press, in the sixteenth century, kings had felt threatened by it. They saw it as a potential weapon of opposition. Many of them tried to ban it. When that didn't work, they tried to control it. Two tactics were granting licenses and subsidies to presses—reserving these, of course, for friendly printers. Another strategy was to make laws punishing criticism of the government that amounted to "seditious libel." The concept was that the king, as source of all justice, ought to be above reproach. Such laws, often used to suppress anti-government opinion, had arrived in America as part of the English legal tradition. And it was against just such a law that Hamilton was making his famous challenge in the Zenger case.

Zenger's jury reached a verdict of "not guilty," setting him free. They had ignored the chief justice's interpretation of the law and accepted that of the defense attorney Hamilton. In effect, the verdict indicated that in a libel case (1) truth is a complete defense and (2) a jury may decide whether the statements are true. Truth as a defense against libel was not upheld as a valid principle of American law for decades afterwards. Yet the Zenger verdict rang out a powerful note for freedom of the press.

POWER OF THE COLONIAL PRESS

And it did not go unheeded. There was a time when colonial newspapers, typically four-page weeklies printed with neither headlines nor illustrations, were tidy and timid. Many were licensed by the royal governors. Usually included were shipping and business news, official government announcements, a few death notices, and lots of advertising. The authorities feared that widespread reading among the people might fan the growing spirit of independence. One governor even bragged that, during his term, there were no printing presses or free schools in his colony.

But populations were expanding, education was improving. And the fires of political strife were flickering up and down the colonies. Encouraged by the Zenger case, the increasingly wealthy class of merchants and landowners began using the press to attack harsh British colonial governments and their Tory supporters. In newspapers, in pamphlets, stirring writers such as Samuel Adams and John Dickinson and Tom Paine sowed the seeds of the American Revolution.

PREFERRED POSITION

> Congress shall make no law . . . abridging the freedom of speech, or of the press; or the right of the people peaceably to assemble, and to petition the government for a redress of grievances.
>
> — 1st Amendment, U.S. Constitution (1791)

When the guns fell silent and Americans began to build a new nation, the adoption in 1791 of the First Amendment (at left) to the Constitution provided a vital guarantee: free expression. It was the initial unit of our Bill of Rights. So precious were the hard-won values of free speech and press and assembly and worship that twentieth-century jurists would speak of their "preferred position" in our system of rights. These by right could be restricted only in the case of grave and immediate dangers.

Americans treasure freedom of expression for many reasons. It fosters a healthy amount of public controversy. It helps the people and their leaders make sound decisions. New ideas can be heard; the better ones can prevail. Bloody conflict is unlikely as long as peaceful change is possible. When criticism is free, better government is frequently the result.

> The [strictest] protection of free speech would not protect a man falsely shouting fire in a theatre and causing a panic.
>
> — Justice Holmes, *Schenck v. United States* (1919)

The First Amendment, however, has never been interpreted to mean that there are no restrictions on speech in this country, that the government had no authority to regulate *any* utterance. For example, fraudulent, or false, statements aimed at cheating persons out of their property traditionally are not protected as free speech. Neither is a conspiracy, or an agreement among persons to commit a crime.

LIBEL

Four major classifications of expression cases have arisen under the First Amendment. The first relates to laws against **libel.** This offense generally includes any false and malicious publication that exposes a person to public hatred, contempt, or ridicule. Libel has traditionally not been protected by the rights of free speech and free press. Following the Zenger case, truth came to be accepted as a complete defense to libel charges.

OBSCENITY

A second class of expression not protected by the First Amendment has been **obscenity,** or pornography—that is, lewd materials that many say cause lust and corrupt public morals. The courts have found it difficult to define what is and what is not obscene. Supporters of anti-obscenity laws, however, offer various arguments for their stand. They claim that such material (1) incites impure sexual thoughts, especially among children; (2) leads to antisocial conduct; and (3) offends many members of the community—as with profanity or public drunkenness.

SUBVERSION

Third, laws regulating **subversion,** an extreme form of dissent, have resulted in controversies over the First Amendment—especially in more recent eras. Historically, the government has sought to suppress criticism in times of crisis. During a period when war between France and the United States seemed likely, in 1798, fear spread that French spies might undermine the government. That year, Congress passed the Alien and Sedition Acts, which fined or imprisoned persons who published "false, scandalous, and malicious" expressions against the government. Many citizens worried that these notorious laws could be misused by the party in power against political opponents. This actually happened when ten editors and printers were suppressed. Because of mounting criticism, the acts were allowed to expire three years later.

But efforts to curb sedition did not die. During the Civil War (1861–1865), Union military authorities silenced many a critical newspaper and its editor—often without trial. During World War I, the Espionage Act of 1917 punished persons who interfered with recruitment. And the Sedition Act of 1918 cracked down on "any disloyal, profane, scurrilous, or abusive language about the form of government of the United States." Then, during World War II, when Germany began rolling up early victories in Europe and Communist-inspired strikes began in this country, Congress passed the Smith Act of 1940. Under this statute, it became a federal crime to preach violent overthrow of the government. Such subversion involved a more specific and radical brand of dissent than mere sedition. Overthrow of the government was a far cry from resistance to the government. But many constitutional questions of free expression remained. In general, what were now the boundaries of lawful dissent?

TIME, PLACE, AND MANNER

In the 1960's, the boundaries of dissent began to be stretched in new directions. Protests grew in scale and frequency. They involved many groups—employee against employer, black against white, student against school, pacifist against recruiting officer. Mass demonstrations poured into the streets and public parks. These forms of protest often went beyond "pure speech." Dissenters used activity, such as marching, picketing, sit-ins, burning images. And they registered their protest by light and sound equipment, by their dress, as well as by dramatic symbols, or signs.

Such forms of dissent opened up a fourth classification of expression cases: **time, place, and manner** problems. The words of the First Amendment protect not only free speech and press, but also "the right of the people peaceably to assemble, and to petition the government for a redress of grievances." Thus, the very activity of an assembly, aside from any speech during the assembly, is protected.

In judging such cases, the elements of time, place, and manner have become increasingly important. The U.S. Supreme Court has attempted to give free expression a high place among the rights granted by the Constitution. But the high bench has also sought to balance this with other community interests that the government has a duty to preserve. Does the demonstration seem in danger of exploding into a riot? Will it unduly interfere with other citizens' peace and quiet? Will a march unduly obstruct the flow of traffic on important thoroughfares?

To make such judgments, the Supreme Court weighs numerous factors. Some of the chief ones have been: (1) whether the apparent purpose of the demonstration is peaceful, (2) the suitability of the place where it takes place, (3) the hostility or friendliness of the spectators, and (4) the ability of police to cope with possible violence.

The Supreme Court has devised numerous tests and formulas to help it decide the cases that follow. But down through the years, the basic question has always been: what are the limits of free expression?

SCHENCK V. UNITED STATES (1919)

In 1917, when the United States entered World War I, its allies seemed in great danger. Offensives begun by the British and the French had been stalled. Russia's government was overthrown, Communist revolutionaries were beginning their takeover of the country, and the Russian war effort was fizzling. Allied shipping had been so hard hit by German submarine attacks that Britain had only a few months' food supplies left.

"Assert your opposition to the draft," cried the leaflet. "Do not submit to intimidation!" Some 15,000 of the leaflets attacking America's entry into World War I were distributed in 1917 to men called to military service.

The leaflet called the draft a "monstrous wrong against humanity that aided Wall Street's chosen few." Its supporters were "cunning politicians" and "a capitalist press." The draft forced American citizens to go overseas and "shoot up people of other lands." The leaflet went on to charge, in fact, that the draft violated the Thirteenth Amendment's ban on slavery. Draftees, it said, were "little better than convicts."

The federal government arrested Charles Schenck, general secretary of the Socialist Party, for printing and giving out the leaflets. It accused him of violating the Espionage Act of 1917—mainly by trying to interfere with recruitment and to stir up defiance of military authority. Schenck was found guilty in a federal district court in Pennsylvania.

His case eventually came before the U.S. Supreme Court. Here Schenck claimed that there was not enough evidence to convict him personally of printing and distributing the leaflets. Anyway, he argued, the leaflets should be protected as free speech.

The government replied that evidence of the trial showed Schenck was in charge of the Socialist Party headquarters from which the leaflets were mailed. Some copies had been found in the inner office. A party report contained a resolution authorizing Comrade Schenck to spend $125 on postage for the leaflets. Furthermore, the govermnent argued that the espionage law was a valid limitation on free speech—and that Schenck, during a time when the country was at war with Germany, had broken that law.

FOR CRITICAL THINKING

The question in every case is whether the words used are used in such circumstances and are of such a nature as to create a clear and present danger. . . .

— Justice Holmes, *Schenck v. United States* (1919)

1. Would you classify this as a libel case; an obscenity case; a subversion case; or a time, place, and manner case? Explain.

2. To what extent do you think that Schenck was responsible for the printing and mailing of the leaflets? What evidence most influenced your answer? Why?

3. To what extent do you think the leaflets would interfere with recruitment of men in World War I? To what extent would the leaflets stir up defiance of military authority? Give reasons for your answers.

4. Can a federal law such as the Espionage Act restrict freedom of speech? Explain. What connection, if any, does the situation of 1917 have to do with your answer?

5. Does the quotation from Justice Holmes (at left) help you solve this case? Explain. Do you think it is from a majority or a dissenting opinion? Why?

6. How do you think the Supreme Court ruled in this case?

SCALES V. UNITED STATES (1961)

Fear of communism has given rise to a long series of First Amendment cases before the Supreme Court. After World War I came the period of the "Red scare." Communists who had overthrown the Russian government in 1917 were now inciting workers around the globe to revolt. Rumors of plots to overthrow the government spread throughout

America. Many states passed anti-revolution laws. In Gitlow v. New York *(1925), the U.S. Supreme Court upheld as constitutional a state law that made it a crime to advocate, or urge, the violent overthrow of organized government. The Court affirmed the conviction of Benjamin Gitlow, a Socialist who printed and distributed a pamphlet urging American workers to strike and join in a revolt to destroy the state. There was no evidence that the pamphlet caused a "clear and present danger" of this actually happening. But the Court said it created a "dangerous tendency" toward an evil the state had a right to prevent.*

Concern about communism in 1940 led Congress to pass the Smith Act, which made it a federal crime to preach forcible overthrow of the government. Using this statute, the Supreme Court in Dennis v. United States *(1951) approved the convictions of eleven top Communists in America. To uphold the Smith Act in general terms, the Court did not use Justice Holmes' "clear and present danger" test from the* Schenck *case or the "dangerous tendency" test from the* Gitlow *case. It used a new test. The seriousness—or "gravity of the evil," said the Court—was important enough here to outweigh the improbability of a Communist revolution. Compare these cases and their tests with the following case.*

Following World War II, in the early days of the Cold War, two young North Carolinians took opposite paths that put them on collision course with each other. One was Junius Irving Scales. Veteran of the Air Force, graduate of the University of North Carolina, he publicly announced in 1946 his membership in the Communist Party, U.S.A. Scales quickly rose to prominence in the party. As a district chairman, he recruited new party members among university students. He furnished them with Communist literature. He instructed them in Communist theory and tactics. And he selected promising members for further training in underground party schools. One day in 1948, he received a fateful postcard from Ralph Clontz, Jr.

Clontz—the other North Carolinian—introduced himself to Scales in the postcard as a Duke University law student interested in communism. This much was true. What he did not reveal was that he had served as a U.S. intelligence officer in Austria and was now an informant for the Federal Bureau of Investigation.

Scales responded to the postcard by mailing Clontz a large box of Communist literature. Shortly afterward, Clontz had dinner at the home of Mr. and Mrs. Scales in Carrboro, North Carolina. From that point on, Clontz penetrated deeper and deeper into the Communist Party. And for the next several years, he reported his findings to the FBI. He said he told Scales that if the Communist Party would educate the American people, they would vote the party into power. Scales replied this was impossible: the government controlled all means of communication and education, as well as the army. Clontz reported that Scales added the "oppressed classes could not be liberated without violent revolution and destruction of the state." According to Clontz, the Party strategy was to unite (1) the working class with (2) the "Negro nation" in the Southern states to prepare for such a revolt.

In 1954, Scales was arrested for violation of the Smith Act of 1940. He was not charged with breaking the act's "advocacy" clause, which made it a federal crime to advocate or preach the overthrow of the government by force. This was the part of the act under which the eleven Communist leaders were convicted in the *Dennis* case. Instead, Scales was accused of violating the "membership" clause of the Smith Act. This punished "whoever organizes or helps or attempts to organize any society, group, or assembly of persons who teach, advocate, or encourage the overthrow or destruction of [the government of the United States or the government of any of its states, territories, districts, or possessions] by force or violence; or becomes or is a member of, or affiliates with, *any such society, group, or assembly of persons, knowing the purposes thereof. . . .*"

Scales objected that the "membership" clause was unconstitutional. He claimed that it punished people for merely joining groups that the government considered dangerous. And he said this was "guilt by association"—violating his right of freedom of speech and especially freedom of assembly.

At the trial in federal district court, the judge instructed the jury that Scales "was an active member of the Party, and not merely a normal, passive, inactive or purely technical member." He added that Scales had "knowledge of the Party's illegal advocacy and a specific intent to bring about violent overthrow as circumstances would permit."

Junius Scales was convicted and sentenced to six years in prison. After a U.S. Court of Appeals affirmed the conviction, the U.S. Supreme Court agreed to review the case.

FOR CRITICAL THINKING

The First Amendment absolutely forbids Congress to outlaw membership in a political party or similar association merely because one of the philosophical tenets of the group is that the existing government should be overthrown by force at some distant time in the future when circumstances may permit.

— Justice Black, *Scales v. United States* (1961)

1. Would you classify this as a libel case; an obscenity case; a subversion case; or a time, place, and manner case. Explain.
2. How do you interpret the "membership" clause of the Smith Act—in your own words? What effect does the phrase "knowing the purposes" have on the requirements for guilt under this clause?
3. Do you agree with Scales' interpretation that this clause allows "guilt by association"? If so, do you think this particular clause would be constitutional or unconstitutional? Why? What part or parts of the Constitution would apply to this problem?
4. Do you agree with the trial judge's instructions that Scales was an *active* member of the Communist Party? What evidence from the case supports your answer? Do you agree with the judge that Scales had both *knowledge* of the party's preaching and a *specific intent* to bring about the violent overthrow of the government? What evidence from the case supports your answer?
5. Using your own interpretation of the "membership" clause, do

you think the language includes active membership?

6. Does the quotation from Justice Black (page 35) help you decide this case? Explain.
7. How do you think the Supreme Court ruled in this case?

GRISWOLD V. CONNECTICUT (1965)

To fight the spread of birth control information, the U.S. Congress in 1873 passed a law outlawing its distribution as a type of lewd and indecent material. This so-called "Comstock Law" was named after Anthony J. Comstock, a New York crusader against vice. Many states afterwards passed "Little Comstock Laws." One was Connecticut. Its 1879 law punished as a criminal offense the use of "any drug, medicinal article or instrument for the purpose of preventing conception." By the 1940's, however, contraceptives—or birth control devices—were being sold in drug stores throughout the state. As the state law was interpreted, these articles could be sold to prevent disease but not to prevent conception. In the 1940's and 1950's, a number of doctors tried to get the Connecticut law repealed. They argued that it deprived many patients of their right to life under the due process clause of the Fourteenth Amendment (page 37). All their efforts failed. Then, in 1961, there erupted this case.

Chill November skies lay over New Haven as police approached the building at 79 Trumbull Street. It was a newly opened free clinic for poor patients operated by the Planned Parenthood League of Connecticut. Inside, the officers received full cooperation from the executive director, Mrs. Estelle Griswold. She explained to them the operations of the clinic. She gave them samples of the birth control literature and devices distributed to married patients by the clinic's staff.

The purpose of the police was to investigate the possible violation of the state's anti-contraceptive law. That was okay with the League. One of its purposes in starting the clinic was to openly violate that very law, make a test case of it, and possibly get it declared unconstitutional.

The clinic's medical director, Dr. C. Lee Buxton, had long tried to get the law repealed. Before this clinic opened, two of his patients had died because of problems connected with their pregnancies. Buxton, a professor of medicine at Yale University, claimed that their lives could have been saved if they had been able to get help from a free birth control clinic. As it was, this was currently the only such clinic in Connecticut. Buxton argued that paying patients often got birth control advice and materials in the privacy of their physicians' offices. But the poor, he said, could turn to no other place than a free clinic for such aid.

Later, police arrested Mrs. Griswold and Dr. Buxton. The two were charged with breaking the following parts of the state code: Section 52–32, General Statutes of Connecticut (1958): "Any person who uses any drug, medical article or instrument for the purpose of preventing conception shall be fined not less than $50 or imprisoned not less than sixty days nor more than one year or be both fined and imprisoned."

Section 54–196: "Any person who assists, abets, counsels, causes, hires, or commands another to commit any offense may be prosecuted as if he were the principal offender."

The first statute was the anti-contraceptive act; the second was a general criminal accessory act.

In the state trial court, three married women patients testified that they had entered the New Haven clinic, where they had received birth control advice and materials that they later used. Mrs. Griswold and Dr. Buxton were found guilty and fined $100 each. Their convictions were affirmed on all appeals in the state courts. Then, in an appeal before the U.S. Supreme Court, attorneys for the defendants included among their arguments:

1. The anti-contraceptive law interfered with the right to free speech protected by the First and the Fourteenth Amendments by preventing the defendants from counseling married couples on birth control.
2. The law also violated the "right to privacy in marriage"—a right not spelled out in the Bill of Rights but guaranteed to the people under the Ninth Amendment and protected against state interference by the Fourteenth.

If the Supreme Court accepted the last argument, it would have to go beyond anything it had decided before. No constitutional "right to privacy" had been previously recognized as an independent principle. In its reply, the State of Connecticut included the following arguments:

1. The defendants could not claim that they had been denied free speech. Dr. Buxton was not using "speech" in practicing medicine at the birth control clinic. Instead, he was taking actions based on his social beliefs. And those actions could be regulated by the state.
2. The defendants were not the proper parties to raise any arguments about a right to privacy in marriage.

FOR CRITICAL THINKING

1. Would you classify this case as libel; obscenity; subversion; time, place and manner; or some other kind of "free expression" problem? Why?

2. Why did Mrs. Griswold cooperate fully with investigating officers?

3. Interpret in your own words the meaning of the two Connecticut statutes with which the defendants were charged. Why were they charged with violating both laws and not just the anti-contraceptive law?

4. Why do you think the defendants argued that the Fourteenth Amendment (at left) applies to this case? What did you learn in the

No state shall . . . deprive any person of life, liberty, or property, without due process of law. . . .

— 14th Amendment, U.S. Constitution (1868)

The enumeration in the Constitution of certain rights shall not be construed to deny or disparage others retained by the people.

— 9th Amendment, U.S. Constitution (1791)

introductory chapter "Constitution, Court, and Legal System" that bears on this question? Do you agree or disagree with the defendants' argument? Why?

5. Do you agree or disagree with the defendants' argument that the Ninth Amendment (at left) guarantees a "right to privacy in marriage" to the people? Why?
6. How do you think the Supreme Court ruled in this case?

TINKER V. DES MOINES SCHOOL DISTRICT (1969)

In 1965 the United States greatly expanded its war effort in Vietnam. It began bombing military and transportation targets inside Communist North Vietnam. And it committed American troops on a broader scale to actively take part in the fighting.

As the conflict dragged on, and as American casualties mounted ever higher, opposition to United States involvement grew at home. Mass demonstrations sprang up, especially on college campuses. Some protesters burned American flags; other young men burned their draft cards. Congress passed a law in 1965 making it a federal crime to forge, alter, or knowingly destroy or mutilate one's draft card. And in United States v. O'Brien *(1968), the U.S. Supreme Court rejected a young draft-card burner's claim that his action was "symbolic speech" protected by the First Amendment. Not all acts used to communicate an idea, said the Court are necessarily protected as free speech. Compare the O'Brien case with the following case.*

Wearing black armbands to protest the Vietnam War was banned in the public schools of Des Moines, Iowa. The school principals in the city had got wind of plans by students to stage such a silent protest at Christmastime. Their official response was swift. Any students wearing armbands to school would be asked to take them off. Should they refuse, they'd be suspended until they removed them.

John Tinker, 15, and his sister, Mary Beth, 13, and their friend, Christopher Eckhardt, 16, knew the risks. They and their parents had met in the Eckhardt home to plan the whole demonstration. By wearing the armbands they would express their opposition to the American war effort in Vietnam—as well as their support for a truce.

On December 16, Christopher and Mary Beth wore their black armbands to school; the next day, John wore his. All three, plus two other students, were suspended and sent home. Their fathers promptly filed a lawsuit in a federal district court. They asked the judge to stop school authorities from suspending these children.

Evidence showed that very few of the 18,000 students of Des Moines had worn the armbands to school. Only five had been suspended. Outside the classroom, a few students had made angry remarks to the armband wearers. But there had been no threats or acts of violence on school grounds. And there was no indication that work at the Des Moines school had been interrupted in any way.

Des Moines school officials did not ban all political symbols. Some students had been allowed to wear political campaign buttons to school. Some had even worn the Iron Cross—considered by them a Nazi symbol. The order banning black armbands did not extend to these other symbols.

The federal district court dismissed the parents' complaint. It ruled that the action of the school officials was lawful. It reflected, said the court, the fear of school officials that a disturbance might erupt in school—because of the widespread controversy over Vietnam. The dismissal was affirmed by a U.S. Court of Appeals. The case then went to the Supreme Court.

FOR CRITICAL THINKING

1. Would you classify this as a libel case; an obscenity case; a subversion case; or a time, place, and manner case?

2. Was the apparent intention of the protesters to stage an orderly or a disorderly demonstration? Explain you answer.

3. To what extent did the wearing of black armbands disrupt the work in the schools?

4. How serious a threat of violence did the reaction of other students or spectators pose to the armband protesters? Explain.

5. Should school officials be able to ban a political expression by students because of fear that it will cause a disturbance? Why?

6. To what extent, if any, should school officials be able to ban one type of political symbol in the schools—and not another?

7. Does the quotation from Justice Fortas (at left) help you solve their case? Explain. Do you think it is from a majority or a dissenting opinion? Why?

8. How do you think the Supreme Court ruled in this case?

First Amendment rights, applied in the light of the special character of the school environment, are available to teachers and students. It can hardly be argued that either students or teachers shed their constitutional rights to freedom of speech or expression at the schoolhouse gate.

— Justice Fortas, *Tinker v. Des Moines School District* (1969)

NEW YORK TIMES V. UNITED STATES (1971)

Opposition to pre-publication government censorship runs deep in Anglo-American legal tradition. It poses a greater threat to freedom of the press than criminal prosecution after publication. From the writings of the eminent English jurist, Sir William Blackstone (see quote, top of page 40), down to the classic Supreme Court case of Near v. Minnesota *in 1931 (see quote, bottom of page 40,) the doctrine against "previous restraints" remained solid. Then, in 1971, the following case rocked the nation. It pitted a presidential administration against two of America's most famous newspapers.*

Sunday's *New York Times,* all 486 pages of it, landed on the nation's doorsteps with its usual thump. There was, however, something highly unusual about this June 13, 1971, issue. A front-page headline read "VIETNAM ARCHIVE: PENTAGON STUDY TRACES 3 DECADES OF GROWING U.S. INVOLVE-

The liberty of the press is indeed essential to the nature of a free state; but this consists in laying no previous restraints upon publications, and not in freedom from censure for criminal matter when published. Every freeman has an undoubted right to lay what sentiments he pleases before the public; to forbid this is to destroy freedom of the press; but if he publishes what is improper, mischievous, or illegal, he must take the consequence of his own temerity. . . .

— Sir William Blackstone, *Commentaries* (1765)

MENT." Thus began a series of articles based on 47 volumes of "top secret" and "secret" papers stolen from the government. It was the biggest, most sensational leak of official documents in the nation's history.

"The Pentagon Papers" captured worldwide attention. No wonder. Compiled by Defense Department analysts, they made up an "inside" history of how the United States had become entangled, deeper and deeper, in the Vietnam War. The 7,000-page study spanned a period from 1945 to 1968, covering administrations of four Presidents—Harry S. Truman, Dwight D. Eisenhower, John F. Kennedy, and Lyndon B. Johnson. Highlights included findings that:

1. The Truman administration had "set" the course of U.S. policy in 1950 by giving military equipment to help France fight Communist forces in its colony of Vietnam.
2. The Eisenhower administration in 1954, after France's defeat and the division of Vietnam into two nations, had played a more "direct role" by (a) deciding to save South Vietnam from Communist takeover, and (b) staging guerrilla attacks against Communist North Vietnam to cripple its war effort.
3. The Kennedy administration had escalated the United States role to one of "broad commitment." The American mission of military advisers to the South Vietnamese was greatly enlarged. American troops began to be used in "combat-support" roles, exposing them increasingly to actual fighting. U.S. officials encouraged a South Vietnamese military group to overthrow their own President Diem, deepening U.S. involvement in the country.
4. The Johnson administration had stepped up secret warfare, including air strikes and commando raids, against North Vietnam in 1964—leading to Communist attacks on American warships in the Gulf of Tonkin. Using previously laid plans, the United States quickly retaliated. Open bombing raids against the North eventually grew to massive levels. And by 1968, a steady buildup of U.S. forces in open warfare caused over half a million Americans to be stationed in South Vietnam.

Liberty of the press, historically considered and taken up by the Federal Constitution, has meant, principally although not exclusively, immunity from previous restraints or censorship.

— Chief Justice Hughes, *Near v. Minnesota* (1931)

On June 13 and 14, *The New York Times* published articles on "The Pentagon Papers." President Richard Nixon's administration reacted strongly. Charging "irreparable injury" to national defense, Attorney General John Mitchell asked a federal district court for an injunction against further publication by the *Times* of official secrets. At the hearing, the government claimed that the *Times* had violated Title 18 U.S. Code, Section 793, a criminal law punishing any person having unauthorized possession of defense information, who "communicates, delivers, transmits [it] to any person not entitled to receive it."

The *Times* argued that this statute had been aimed by Congress against espionage or spying—not against publishing by the

The President shall be commander-in-chief of the Army and Navy of the United States, and of the militia of the several states, when called into the actual service of the United States. . . .

— Article II, Section 2, U.S. Constitution

press. Applying such a law to a newspaper, contended the *Times*, would amount to an unprecedented "prior restraint" of the type banned by *Near v. Minnesota* (1931). Meanwhile, *The Washington Post* had begun to publish its own articles on "The Pentagon Papers." So had hundreds of other newspapers. The government filed lawsuits against the *Post* and a few others. But the *Times* complained to the judge that an injunction was now meaningless and that its readers "alone in this country are being deprived of the story." The federal district judge in New York ruled against the government. A U.S. Court of Appeals, however, held up publication of some documents which, said the government, posed a "grave and immediate danger" to national security.

The case of the *Times* and the *Post* was sped to the U.S. Supreme Court where it was argued in emergency overtime sessions. Attacking "government censorship," the papers said they derived their right to publish this historic material from the public's right to know under the First Amendment. The government countered that "the First Amendment was not intended to make it possible for the executive . . . to protect the security of the United States." It added that the general powers of the President, under the original Constitution, to conduct the nation's military affairs (see quote, upper left) and its foreign affairs (see quote, lower left) should be interpreted to limit the specific guarantees of the Bill of Rights adopted later. In less than a week, the Supreme Court heard and decided this heated case, one that would normally take months to process.

[The President] shall have power, by and with the advice and consent of the Senate, to make treaties [as well as] nominate and . . . appoint ambassadors, other public ministers and consuls . . . of the United States. . . .

— Article II, Section 2, U.S. Constitution

FOR CRITICAL THINKING

1. Would you classify this as a libel case; an obscenity case; a subversion case; a time, place, and manner case; or other type of free expression case? Explain.
2. Under Section 793, should the words "communicates, delivers, transmits" be interpreted to also mean "publishes"? Explain.
3. Does the quote from Justice Stewart (page 45) help you decide this case? Is it from a majority or a dissenting opinion? Why?
4. How do you think the Supreme Court ruled in this case?

MILLER V. CALIFORNIA (1973)

Government efforts to control printed and pictorial material dealing with sex and sexual morality began in this country during the 1800's. The first federal statute was the Tariff Act of 1842, which banned the import of "obscene" prints and pictures. By the mid-twentieth century, however, despite state and federal laws, pornography had become big business in cities and suburbs. Mail-order houses peddling "sexploitation" books and magazines and records, "adult bookstores," and "skin flick" cinemas were raking in large sales.

In Roth v. United States *(1957), the U.S. Supreme Court considered for the first time whether a person could sell pornographic, or obscene, materials under the protection of the First Amendment. Obscenity was not protected free expression, ruled the Court. It held in the* Roth *case that the "proper definition of obscenity" was "whether to the average person, applying contemporary community standards, the dominant theme of the material taken as a whole appeals to the prurient [obsessively lewd] interest." In later decisions, the Supreme Court added other tests. Material is obscene (a) "if it is patently offensive" because it affronts today's community standards on "the description or representation of sexual matters" and (b) if the material "is utterly without redeeming social value." Then came the following case.*

A curious envelope arrived at a restaurant in Newport Beach, California. The owner and his mother in the Pacific Coast resort town were opening the day's mail. This particular envelope looked for all the world like unsolicited advertising. It was. The contents, however, were not the day-to-day type. Inside were five heavily illustrated brochures advertising four sex books and a film. There was some descriptive text. But the brochures mostly contained explicit pictures showing people engaged in a number of sex acts.

The restaurant owner and his mother, complaining that they were offended by the brochures, turned them over to the police. Officers then arrested Marvin Miller, a California book distributor who had sent the brochures as part of a mass mailing campaign. Miller was charged with violating the following sections of the state criminal code:

Section 311.2: "Every person who knowingly sends or causes to be sent, or brings or causes to be brought, into this state for sale or distribution, or in this state prepares, publishes, prints, exhibits, distributes, or offers to distribute, or has in his possession with intent to distribute, any obscene matter, is guilty of a misdemeanor."

Section 311 (a): "Obscene means that to the average person, applying contemporary standards, the predominant appeal of the matter, taken as a whole, is to prurient interest, that is, a shameful or morbid interest in nudity [or] sex . . . which goes substantially beyond customary limits of candor in description or representation of such matters and is matter which is utterly without redeeming social importance."

At the trial in Los Angeles, a police officer testified as an "expert witness" on how the community felt about the brochures. With years of specialization in obscenity cases, he had conducted a statewide survey on what various communities considered to be obscene material. He had testified as an "expert witness" 26 times in the year before the Miller trial. In his opinion, the Miller brochures were "obscene."

The trial judge instructed the jury that in determining whether the "dominant theme of the material as a whole . . . appeals to the prurient interest" and in determining whether the material "goes substantially beyond customary limits of candor and affronts contemporary community standards of decency," it should apply "contemporary community standards of the state of California."

The trial jury convicted Miller. On appeal, which eventually came before the U.S. Supreme Court, his attorneys included among their arguments the following points:

1. The application of local or state standards, rather than a national one, violated the First and the Fourteenth Amendments. Standards would vary from place to place. And some sellers—unwilling to risk criminal prosecution—might use standards overrestrictive for their community and avoid distributing otherwise protected materials. Thus, a kind of censorship would be imposed on many communities—and this is prohibited by the Bill of Rights.
2. The application of varying state and local standards would also obstruct the free flow of interstate commerce.

FOR CRITICAL THINKING

1. Would you classify this case as libel; obscenity; subversion; time, place and manner; or some other kind of "free expression" problem? Why?
2. Do you think Sections 311.2 and 311(a) of the California criminal code meet the tests of obscenity outlined by the U.S. Supreme Court in the *Roth* and other cases that preceded the *Miller* case? Explain.
3. Do you agree or disagree with the defense argument that a national standard of obscenity should be applied—rather than state or local ones? Why?
4. Do you agree or disagree with all the tests of obscenity outlined by the Supreme Court prior to the *Miller* case? Why? How hard do you think it would be, using all these tests, for the state to prove a particular book or film or advertising brochure was "obscene?" Explain.
5. How do you think the Supreme Court ruled in this case?

HAZELWOOD SCHOOL DISTRICT V. KUHLMEIER (1988)

*In recent years the question of students' rights has been hotly debated. In 1985 the Supreme Court ruled that the Fourth Amendment does not protect students from "unreasonable searches" in the same way that it protects adults. The Court said that school officials who suspect that students have drugs may search student lockers and purses (*New Jersey v. T.L.O.*). The next year the justices ruled that a student may be suspended for giving a speech during a school assembly that school officials consider offensive (*Bethel School District No. 403 v. Fraser*). Then in 1988 came the following censorship case.*

When Cathy Kuhlmeier opened her latest issue of *Spectrum,* the high school newspaper, she was amazed. Instead of the normal six pages that she and her fellow editors at Hazelwood East High

School had prepared, the paper had only four pages. What had happened to the missing pages? She would soon find out.

The deleted pages contained six articles, two of which Robert Reynolds, the principal at the Missouri high school, considered inappropriate. One article was about divorce. It named a student who complained bitterly about her father. The other article was about teenage pregnancy. In addition to factual information on teen pregnancy, there were personal accounts written by three students. There was nothing sexually explicit in their accounts, though the students did tell of their experiences with sex and birth control. The students were unnamed but possibly they were identifiable.

Reynolds wanted to protect the rights of the father who had not been given a chance to respond to his daughter's criticism. He also wanted to protect the privacy of the three unnamed students. Finally, the principal believed that references to sexual activity were inappropriate for younger students who would read the newspaper.

The principal believed there was no time to make the necessary changes in the stories before the scheduled press run. If he held up publication, the newspaper would not appear before the end of the school year. Therefore, he concluded, his only choice was to approve publication of a four-page newspaper, eliminating the two pages in which the articles appeared.

Cathy Kuhlmeier and two fellow editors charged that the principal's action amounted to censorship. Believing that he had violated their First Amendment rights of free speech, they took their case to court. There they argued that *Spectrum* was not only a school paper but also a "public forum." As such, the principal could only censor articles that would have disrupted classwork or caused disorder in school. Neither of the articles in question, they contended, would have done so.

Hazelwood School District responded that the Board of Education allocated funds from its annual budget for the printing of *Spectrum.* Those funds were supplemented by proceeds from sales of the paper. The printing expenses during the most recent school year totaled $4,668.50; revenue from sales was $1,166.84. The Board paid all other costs associated with the newspaper—supplies, textbooks, and a portion of a journalism teacher's salary.

A Federal Appeals Court agreed with the students, holding that school officials had violated their rights by deleting the two pages from the newspaper. Hazelwood School District appealed to the U.S. Supreme Court.

The question whether the First Amendment requires a student to tolerate particular speech—the question we addressed in Tinker—is different from the question whether the First Amendment requires a school affirmatively to promote particular student speech.

— Justice White, *Hazelwood School District v. Kuhlmeier* (1988)

FOR CRITICAL THINKING

1. Do you think there should be any limits on what a school newspaper can publish? Explain.
2. The school both sponsored and helped finance the student paper.

Should those facts play an important part in the decision? Why or why not?

3. Do you think student speech should be restricted more than the speech of citizens generally? Why or why not?
4. Does the quote from Justice White (page 44) help you decide the case? Is it from a majority or a dissenting opinion? Why?
5. How do you think the Supreme Court ruled in this case?

EXPLORING THE MAIN IDEAS

WHAT DO YOU THINK?

Illustration Review

Now that you have finished this chapter's cases, re-analyze the pictures on pages 26–27. Which cases relate to which pictures? In what ways, if any, would your answers to the questions in "Illustration Analysis" at the beginning of the chapter now change? In what ways, if any, would your answers remain the same?

1. Which of the following formulas mentioned in the materials of *Schenck v. United States* and *Scales v. United States* do you think is the most helpful in distinguishing lawful dissent from illegal subversion: (a) the clear and present danger test, (b) the dangerous tendency test, (c) the gravity of the evil test? Explain your answer.
2. Which of the cases in this chapter do you believe to be the most just? Which do you believe to be the most unjust? Which do you think will have the greatest impact on problems confronting America today? Explain your answers.
3. Based on your own knowledge and what you have learned in this chapter, how much freedom of expression do you think exists in America today? Explain your answer.

THINGS TO DO

In the absence of the governmental checks and balances present in other areas of our national life, the only effective restraint upon executive policy and power in the areas of national defense and international affairs may lie in an enlightened citizenry—in an informed and critical public opinion which alone can here protect the values of democratic government. For this reason, it is perhaps here that a press that is alert, aware, and free most vitally serves the basic purpose of the First Amendment.

— Justice Stewart, *New York Times v. United States* (1971)

1. Using encyclopedias, history texts, and any other sources your teacher may suggest, write an essay comparing the dangers of the times out of which the *Schenck* case and the *Scales* case grew. In your paper state whether you believe these dangers justified the governmental limitation on free speech in each case. And give reasons for your statements.
2. Choose a fact-finding committee to obtain from a city official suggested by your teacher a copy of the laws in your city relating to demonstrations in public streets and parks. Elect another committee to analyze these laws according to the principles developed in this chapter and to report their findings to the class. Discuss their findings as a class. The class should then try to decide which, if any, of the laws it believes should be changed.
3. Using the procedures outlined in the back of this book, put on a mock trial of the *Tinker* case.

3 Separation of Powers

The final days of John Adams as second President of the United States were hectic. A Congress controlled by his fellow party members, the Federalists, had passed last-minute laws that awaited his signature. Among them was legislation giving him the power to name as many justices of the peace for the nation's capitol as he wished. Around the first of March, 1801, with less than a week to serve as President, Adams appointed 42 men to

Illustration Analysis

Analyze the pictures on pages 46-47. Why do you think the design includes the illustration of a B-52 bomber? How does it relate to this chapter's title? Which banch or branches of U.S. government has control of such power? Why do you think the design includes the photograph of a dam? What do symbols of TVA and NRA stand for? With what period of United States history are they identified? Why do you think the tape recorder is included in the design? With what event in American history is it associated? What message, if any, does this design communicate by overlapping all motifs with the American flag?

these posts. The Senate confirmed them. To make the appointments legal, the President had to sign written commissions for each, his Secretary of State had to stamp them with the Great Seal of the United States, and government officers had to deliver them. These steps took time and, in the last-minute rush, not all of the commissions were delivered. This minor slip-up set the stage for a controversial case that profoundly affected the future of the Supreme Court.

The newly elected Thomas Jefferson succeeded Adams as President. When Jefferson's party, initially called the Democratic Republicans and much later, simply the Democrats, took control of Congress, they wasted no time in abolishing most of the new court positions created by the Federalists. And they refused to deliver some of the commissions that the Adams administration had processed. Federalists strongly protested; and the dispute, because many of the appointments had been signed at the eleventh hour, was called the case of the "midnight judges."

Four of the men denied commissions, led by William Marbury, complained to the U.S. Supreme Court. They demanded a *writ of mandamus*—a court order compelling a public official to carry out a given duty. They wanted the writ to order the Republican Secretary of State, James Madison, to deliver their commissions. These appointees claimed that the Supreme Court had the "original jurisdiction" to try this case and issue the writ. To support their argument, they cited the Judiciary Act of 1789 (see quote, page 49).

Marbury and the others put the Supreme Court on the spot. The Court was a Federalist stronghold. Its Chief Justice was the Federalist, John Marshall—the former Secretary of State in the Adams administration who, ironically, had failed to have Marbury's commission delivered.

Political controversy boiled over the case. Marshall knew that if the Court ordered Secretary of State Madison to deliver the commissions, the Republican Congress might try to impeach some of the Court's members. There was also the possibility that Republican officials simply would refuse to obey the Court's writ. Either action would seriously threaten the prestige of the Supreme Court.

The Marshall Court directed Secretary of State Madison to introduce evidence at its next session stating why the writ should not be issued. Madison and other members of the Jefferson administration simply ignored the Court's demand. Meanwhile, the Republican Congress passed a law postponing the next session of the Supreme Court for more than a year.

In February, 1803, when the Court next convened, it heard the case of *Marbury v. Madison.* At the hearing, it was brought out that the Adams administration had taken all the steps required by law that normally would have entitled Marbury to his commission. The crucial question was the one of original jurisdiction. Did the Court have the power to try this case and to issue a writ of mandamus?

In all cases affecting ambassadors, other public ministers, and consuls, and those in which a state shall be a party, the Supreme Court shall have original jurisdiction.

— Article III, Section 2, Clause 2, U.S. Constitution

Chief Justice Marshall knew that he had to consider not only the Judiciary Act of 1789 but also Article III, Section 2, of the Constitution itself (see quote at left). Practically speaking, however, the problem was whether the Court should risk taking a stand that would be challenged by the Republicans. What would happen if it issued a ruling that the Jefferson administration refused to obey? Could the Court survive such damage to its prestige? Regardless of the merits of Marbury's request, would it be better to protect the Court by avoiding a direct clash? Clearly, the Chief Justice faced a hard decision. He had to decide which was more important: upholding individual rights, or the survival of the Court.

IN YOUR OPINION

1. Do you think the words "other public ministers" refer only to foreign diplomatic officials or to a broad category of public officials, domestic as well as foreign, in which are included the justices of the peace in *Marbury v. Madison*?
2. What conflict, if any, do you see between Article III, Section 2, of the Constitution and the Judiciary Act of 1789 passed by Congress? If you believe that conflict exists, how would you have Chief Justice Marshall resolve it?
3. What bearing, if any, do you think Article VI, Section 2, of the Constitution (see quote below) should have on this case? Why?
4. When a provision of the Constitution and a statute passed by Congress are in conflict, which do you think should generally prevail? Give reasons for your answer.
5. Which do you think should generally prevail when a provision of the Constitution and a statute passed by a state legislature are in conflict? Give reasons for your answer.
6. Which do you think should generally prevail when a federal law and a state law are in conflict? Give reasons for your answer.

The Supreme Court . . . shall have power to issue . . . writs of mandamus, in casses warranted by the principles and usages of law, to any courts appointed, or persons holding office, under the authority of the United States.

— Judiciary Act of 1789

CORNERSTONE OF THE SUPREME COURT

Before the *Marbury* case, the U.S. Supreme Court won little glory or even attention. It had heard very few cases, let alone important ones. Its first Chief Justice, John Jay, resigned in 1795 to become governor of New York. The man nominated to be his successor, John Rutledge, was rejected by the Senate. Oliver Ellsworth was confirmed but resigned after serving only four years.

Then came John Marshall. Behind his careless dress, his genial manner, was a brilliant mind and a persuasive personality. Appointed Chief Justice while serving as Secretary of State in the Adams administration, the eloquent Federalist from Virginia dominated the Supreme Court for 34 years. The vision, the logic of his decisions established the influence of the Court. He made it co-equal with the presidency and the Congress.

The Constitution, and the laws of the United States which shall be made in pursuance thereof; and all treaties made, or which shall be made under the authority of the United States, shall be the supreme law of the land. . . .

— Article VI, Section 2, U.S. Constitution

MARSHALL AND THE MIDNIGHT JUDGES

The first of Marshall's great decisions was *Marbury v. Madison.* In it, he announced the right of the Supreme Court to rule an act of Congress unconstitutional. When such a statute was in conflict with the Constitution, the Supreme Court could rule it null and void. This was new; it was sweeping. Nowhere did the Constitution expressly give the Supreme Court this power. Marshall would have to establish it by reasoning.

THE FUNDAMENTAL LAW

John Marshall very carefully analyzed the case in terms of three questions. First, did Marbury have a legal right to his commission as a justice of the peace? *Yes.* Second, if he had a right, and that right had been violated, was there a legal remedy? *Yes.* Third, could the Supreme Court decree the proper remedy, a writ of mandamus? *No.*

To reach this conclusion, the Chief Justice first declared the Court's right to interpret laws. "It is emphatically the province . . . of the judicial department to say what the law is." Then he interpreted Article III, Section 2, of the Constitution (see quote, page 49) in a narrow, literal way. He said that Section 2 granted the Supreme Court original jurisdiction only in those instances expressly listed. The writ of mandamus was not among them. Therefore, the attempt by the Judiciary Act of 1789 (see quote, page 49) to extend the Court's original jurisdiction including such a writ stood in direct conflict with the Constitution itself. So the statute was of no effect.

BIRTH OF JUDICIAL REVIEW

Thus, the Federalist Chief Justice had neatly sidestepped his political dilemma. By not issuing the writ requested by the Federalist Marbury, he had given the Republicans the final result they sought. And in doing that, he even limited the original jurisdiction of his court. Far more important, however, this bold and able jurist had managed to lay down the very cornerstone of the Supreme Court's great powers. This cornerstone is called **judicial review.** It includes the Court's authority to interpret the Constitution. It includes the authority to apply a statute and to decide whether it violates the Constitution.

Using the concept of judicial review, Chief Justice Marshall and his nationalistic court, in decision after decision, staked out ever-broader boundaries of federal power. In *Fletcher v. Peck* (1810), he held that the Supreme Court could declare a state statute unconstitutional. In *Cohens v. Virginia* (1821), he held that the high bench could overturn the rulings of state courts involving federal questions. These cases, as well as *Marbury,* reflected the **supremacy clause** of the Constitution (see lower quote on page 49).

There is certainly nothing in the circumstances under which our constitution was formed; nothing in the history of the times, which would justify the opinion that the confidence reposed in the States was so implicit as to leave in them and their tribunals the power of resisting or defeating, in the form of law, the legitimate measures of the Union.

— Chief Justice Marshall, *Cohens v. Virginia* (1821)

SEPARATION OF POWERS

The concept of judicial review was a logical extension of our constitutional system based on **separation of powers.** The makers of the Constitution gave the power to make laws to the legislative branch of the federal government; the power to administer the laws, to the executive branch; and the power to interpret laws, to the judicial branch. "All legislative powers herein granted shall be vested in a Congress of the United States," says Article I of the Constitution. "The executive power shall be vested in a President of the United States of America," says Article II. "The judicial power of the United States," says Article III, "shall be vested in one Supreme Court, and in such inferior courts as the Congress may from time to time ordain and establish."

The framers of the Constitution purposely built a system on separation of powers because history and their colonial experience had taught them to fear a strong, centralized government. They aimed to prevent the same officials from making the laws, carrying them out, and judging their meaning. They did not want the President of the United States to dominate the legislative or the judicial branches. Nor did they want either of those branches to dominate the President in the legitimate pursuit of his constitutional powers and duties.

The Constitution did not specifically state that the Supreme Court had the final authority to declare acts of the other federal branches, as well as of state governments, unconstitutional. Rather it was the reasoned interpretation of the Marshall Court that began the concept of judicial review, which has become so fundamental to our entire legal structure today.

LIMITATIONS ON REVIEW

The power of judicial review was not without limits. The Supreme Court could not pick any law out of the air and determine its constitutionality. Rather, the law would have to come before the Court in a "case or controversy." That is, the case must have been properly brought into court by persons having a legal interest in the matter.

Over the years, some members of the Supreme Court developed still another limitation: the theory of **judicial restraint.** Their view was that courts ought to defer to a legislature's decision—as long as it was not unreasonable—in fixing the boundaries of personal freedom. After all, according to this theory, elected representatives are closer to the people than are Supreme Court justices. Therefore they should be more perceptive in balancing the competing interests of society in a given conflict. In the case of a demonstration, for example, Supreme Court justices must be mindful of the need to balance the rights of demonstrators to gather peacefully with the community's right to unobstructed motor traffic within its boundaries.

INDUSTRIAL REVOLUTION

The Congress shall have power . . . to regulate commerce with foreign nations, and among the several states. . . .

— Article I, Section 8, U.S. Constitution

After the *Marbury* case, the Court did not declare another act of Congress unconstitutional for a half-century—until the eve of the Civil War. And after the war, the Court used the Constitution's **commerce clause** (see quote at left) to uphold acts of Congress that greatly expanded federal power in this area.

The last half of the nineteenth century in America belonged to the Industrial Revolution. Factories mushroomed in the cities. Immigrants poured in to work the assembly lines. They used standard parts in mass-producing goods faster and cheaper than ever before. The goods, clattering over the lengthening tracks of America's railroads, reached ever broader markets. Big companies made big profits, enticed more money from investors, developed newer products—and grew still bigger.

PANICS, DEPRESSIONS, AND MONOPOLIES

Industrial progress, however, was accompanied by a series of ups and downs. Financial panic rocked the country in 1873, in 1893, and worst of all, in the grim years after the Great Crash of 1929. In the depressions that followed the panics, demand for goods and services declined. Prices and profits fell. Businesses failed. Unemployment soared.

The path out of a depression was frequently long and bumpy. Bigger, more powerful firms swallowed up weaker ones. Such mergers often led to giant monopolies. Some dominated entire industries. Unhampered by strong competition, monopolies raised prices on their products. Higher prices hurt the individual consumer, who had to pay—or do without.

GOVERNMENT AND THE COMMERCE POWER

Government began to step in. Because many giant-sized industrial problems were not limited to a single state, the federal government came to play an increasingly stronger role. Congress passed the Interstate Commerce Act in 1887 to regulate the rates charged by railroads, telegraph companies, and other big interstate firms. And, in 1890, Congress enacted the Sherman Anti-Trust Act—prohibiting interstate companies from establishing monopolies.

Both statutes were based on the commerce clause. Throughout the history of the Supreme Court, interpretation of this clause has progressively broadened in scope. In recent decades, it has been used to justify almost every federal regulation of interstate business transactions. The Court has declared that "commerce" includes the transportation of people as well as goods; the sale of television and film rights; the sending of stock market quotations by telegraph. The power to "regulate" includes the authority to restrain or completely stop.

BALANCE OF POWERS

In this chapter, we will dig into pivotal Supreme Court cases that analyze the long struggle in America for governmental power. Under the Constitution, powers have been parceled out to the various branches and levels of government. None is without limits. In these cases, the emphasis will be placed on the boundaries of power: between one federal branch and another, between federal and state governments, between government and private industry.

The cases reveal how the great government institutions clash as they seek more power. Trends will show how the boundaries change from time to time. And throughout this chapter, the focus will be on the Supreme Court in its role as a national policymaker—dealing with great and urgent issues, weighing one governmental force against another, ever seeking to preserve the constitutional balance of power.

McCULLOCH V. MARYLAND (1819)

The power struggle between those who wanted a strong central government and those who wanted strong state governments dominated the early history of the United States. Each side sought to have the Constitution interpreted in a way that favored its own interests. The advocates of strong central government were known first as Federalists and later as Whigs. These "loose constructionists" placed the broadest possible interpretation on the powers—both expressed and implied—given by the Constitution to the federal government. Those who favored strong state governments were the Democratic-Republicans (later the Democrats). These "strict constructionists" interpreted the expressed and implied powers of the federal government as narrowly as possible.

A heated debate broke out in the First Congress (1789–1791), eventually growing so sharp that it led to the new nation's first political parties, the Federalists and the Democratic-Republicans. The rift occurred over whether to create a national bank.

The first national bank was chartered in 1791 to provide a safe place to deposit federal government funds and to issue money with the same value in every state. When its twenty-year charter expired in 1811, Congress battled long and hard over whether to charter a Second Bank of the United States. Finally, in 1816, Congress approved the second charter.

Those who wished to enlarge state powers had failed in their effort to keep the national government out of the banking business. States particularly resented the federal bank's competing with their own state-chartered banks.

In 1818 the Maryland legislature passed a law to penalize banks operating in the state without a Maryland charter. This penalty took the form of a tax on the bank notes issued by such a bank. The law obviously was aimed at the Baltimore branch of the Second Bank of the United States.

Ignoring the Maryland law, the Baltimore branch continued to issue bank notes without paying the tax. The state then filed a lawsuit against the cashier of the Baltimore branch, James William McCulloch. When a U.S. Court of Appeals upheld Maryland's right to collect taxes from the Second Bank, the federal government sought review by the Supreme Court.

The federal government claimed that the Maryland law was not constitutional. This argument maintained that the tax law was clearly designed to interfere with the operation of a federally chartered bank—a bank established by federal law.

Maryland questioned the power of the federal government to establish banks. No such power had been delegated by the Constitution. Lawyers for the State of Maryland concluded that no such power could or should be implied.

FOR CRITICAL THINKING

1. Would you classify this case as an interstate commerce case, a state "police powers" case, or a "balance of powers" case? Why?
2. How do you think the framers of the Constitution would feel about a state taxing a federal institution like the army, the navy, or post offices? Why?
3. Does the quotation from Chief Justice Marshall (at left) help you decide this case? Explain. Do you think it is from a majority or a dissenting opinion? Why?
4. How do you think the Supreme Court ruled in this case?

The power to tax involves the power to destroy.

— Chief Justice Marshall, *McCulloch v. Maryland* (1819)

GIBBONS V. OGDEN (1824)

Most early attempts to develop a steamboat ended in failure. More successful in using a steam engine to propel a vessel were Robert R. Livingston and Robert Fulton. Their Clermont *really opened the era of steam-powered navigation as it made the round trip between New York City and Albany in August of 1807. It also set the stage for one of the pivotal cases of the Marshall Court.*

To encourage development of a commercially successful steamboat, the New York legislature in 1803 granted a monopoly—or exclusive right—to operate such boats in state-controlled waters. The holders of the monopoly were Livingston and Fulton. The two built a number of steamboats after the *Clermont;* they also formed steamboat companies. Because of their monopoly, every steamboat in New York waters had to be operated or licensed by them.

New York's steamboat monopoly angered other states. Free trade was seriously threatened when other states began to grant similar monopolies. Soon Livingston and Fulton became involved in an endless series of lawsuits. They sought court orders against those who violated their monopoly.

The legal showdown involved Aaron Ogden, a man who had obtained his shipping rights from the Livingston-Fulton monopoly. A former New Jersey governor, Ogden in 1815 had obtained from the Livingston interests a ten-year monopoly on steamship service between Elizabethtown Point, New Jersey, and New York City. Three years later he had to fight in court to protect those rights.

Thomas Gibbons of Georgia, a former business partner of Ogden, had started a competing ferry service on the Elizabethtown-New York City route. Gibbons ignored Ogden's monopoly rights. To protect these, however, Ogden asked the New York courts to issue an order stopping Gibbons' ferry service. Gibbons countered that his shipping privilege had been granted under the Federal Coasting Act of 1793. The New York courts ruled in favor of Ogden.

Gibbons appealed to the U.S. Supreme Court. Here he argued that the states had no right to regulate commerce between the states. The Constitution, he said, had clearly given this power to Congress.

Plaintiff Ogden, in turn, argued that the right of Congress to regulate interstate commerce did not apply. New York State, he said, had done nothing to interfere with commerce. The monopoly on operating steamboats regulated navigation rather than commerce.

FOR CRITICAL THINKING

The Congress shall have power . . . to regulate commerce with foreign nations, and among the several states. . . .

— Article I, Section 8, U.S. Constitution

1. Would you classify this case as an interstate commerce case, a state "police powers" case, or a "balance of powers" case? Why?
2. Read the commerce clause of the Constitution at left. To whom does it give the power to regulate foreign and interstate commerce? How would you define interstate commerce? What does it include? Give some examples.
3. Do you think that the grant of a monopoly for the operation of steamboats in New York waters was an attempt to regulate interstate commerce? Explain.
4. Did the monopoly granted by New York State interfere with any law passed by Congress? If not, tell why not. If it did, name the federal law—and explain how the interference occurred.
5. How do you think the Supreme Court ruled in this case?

SCHECHTER POULTRY CORPORATION V. UNITED STATES (1935)

Following the stock market crash of 1929, the American economy plummeted downhill toward ruin. Businesses failed. Banks closed. Eventually, more than thirteen milllion persons—one out of every four workers—lost their jobs. In 1933 the newly inauguarated Democratic

President, Franklin D. Roosevelt, and his "New Deal" administration reacted swiftly to this Great Depression crisis. During an emergency special session called the "Hundred Days," they herded through Congress a flurry of complex and sweeping laws. These were designed to revive and regulate industry, banking, and agriculture.

The most far-reaching—as well as the most controversial—measure to emerge from the "Hundred Days" was the National Industrial Recovery Act (NIRA). This key New Deal law was intended to revive industry and as a result to insure employment for jobless workers. It sought to check competition within industries by substituting self-regulating partnerships of business, labor, and government. The act called for each industry, under the supervision of a federal agency called the National Recovery Administration, to adopt a "code of fair practices."

Groups of business leaders from each industry hurried to Washington, D.C., to write these codes—setting prices, standards, and quotas for their products. Most of the codes outlawed child labor and set maximum hours and minimum wages for adults. Provisions of the codes were enforceable by federal law.

Within several months, 95 percent of the nation's industries had adopted codes. Among the more than 800 codes approved by the NRA was the "Live Poultry Code." It covered the poultry industry in the greater New York City area. Among its various provisions, this code required inspections, periodic sales reports, and the licensing of all poultry dealers.

The Live Poultry Code was for the most part ignored by the A.L.A. Schechter Poultry Corporation and the Schechter Live Poultry Market, wholesale dealers in Brooklyn. In 1935 and 1936, the two companies spent a great deal of time contesting the provisions in court. They were convicted in federal court of 18 violations of the code. Because one of the charges involved the sale of an unfit chicken, the case became popularly known as the "Sick Chicken Case."

Because the "Sick Chicken Case" raised some serious and urgent issues during these hard times, it eventually reached the U.S. Supreme Court. Here, the Schechter companies argued that the National Industrial Recovery Act, under which this code was adopted, permitted "an unconstitutional delegation by Congress of legislative power." The companies also charged that the NIRA attempted to regulate intrastate commerce—"which lay outside the [constitutional] authority of Congress."

The heart of the New Deal's effort to bring American industry back to life was under constitutional attack. Federal lawyers argued that the Supreme Court should view the NIRA "in the light of the grave national crisis with which Congress was confronted." This crisis had demanded, the government claimed, the broadest possible cooperation by those engaged in the various trades and industries.

Answering the intrastate regulation charge, the government said that most of the poultry sold by the Schechter companies came from other states. Thus the poultry was in the "flow" of interstate commerce. Furthermore, contended the government, even if the Schechter business were entirely intrastate, it "affected" interstate commerce—and, therefore, could be regulated by Congress.

FOR CRITICAL THINKING

1. Would you classify this case as an interstate commerce case, a state "police powers" case, or a "balance of powers" case? Why?
2. Under the National Industrial Recovery Act (NIRA), who had the power to write codes such as the Live Poultry Code? What branch of the federal government approved the codes? To what extent, if any, did these codes have the force of federal law? Explain your answer.
3. Would you agree or disagree with the government's argument that Schechter's business was in the "flow" of interstate commerce, that it "affected" interstate commerce—and, therefore, that it was subject to federal regulation? Explain the position or positions that you take.
4. Do you think the Supreme Court, in deciding this case, should have taken into account the great economic crisis that confronted Congress when it passed the NIRA? Explain.
5. Does the quotation from Chief Justice Hughes (at left) help you solve this case? Explain. Do you think it is from a majority or a dissenting opinion? Why?
6. How do you think the Supreme Court ruled in the case?

> Extraordinary conditions may call for extraordinary remedies. But the argument necessarily stops short of an attempt to justify action which lies outside the sphere of constitutional authority. Extraordinary conditions do not create or enlarge constitutional power.
>
> — Chief Justice Hughes, *Schechter Poultry Corp. v. United States* (1935)

ASHWANDER V. TVA (1936)

As America began its long, slow climb out of the Great Depression, the initial broad approval of the New Deal weakened. A growing number of critics began calling President Roosevelt's policies radical and unconstitutional. This new mood was also reflected in the Supreme Court. By a narrow margin it had upheld some anti-Depression statutes when Chief Justice Charles Evans Hughes and Associate Justice Owen J. Roberts joined the Court's three liberals. Together, they had outvoted a solid block of four conservatives. Then, in 1935 and 1936, Hughes and Roberts began siding the other way. The Court struck down such important New Deal measures as the NIRA, the Railroad Retirement Act, and the Agricultural Adjustment Act.

About this time, the court heard the following controversial case. And it was not long afterward that Roosevelt unveiled his plan to reorganize the Court. Opponents attacked this as a "court-packing" scheme. Its aim was to get a friendly majority on the bench by persuading Congress to let him appoint additional judges.

A stormy dispute broke out over the Tennessee Valley Authority Act. One of the most revolutionary New Deal measures enacted by Congress during the "Hundred Days" in 1933, it gave the national government unprecedented powers in a seven-state area. The new law called for a federal agency, the Tennessee Valley Authority (TVA), to build dams, to generate and sell electricity—as well as to conduct vast, long-range navigation, irrigation, flood control, and reforestation projects—throughout the 40,000 square-mile watershed of the Tennessee River and its tributaries.

Conservatives were outraged. To them, the TVA legislation raised the red flag of socialism. The federal government would enter the business of generating electricity in a big way. Moreover, it would sell electricity at reduced rates in direct competition with privately owned power companies—thus forcing them to cut their rates and, as a result, their profits.

A small group of conservative stockholders in a private utility company attacked the constitutionality of TVA; they demanded that the federal district court stop its operations. Led by George Ashwander, these stockholders of the Alabama Power Company had tried unsuccessfully to prevent this company from doing business with TVA. The district court's ruling was fundamentally in favor of Ashwander and his group. The TVA appealed to a U.S. Court of Appeals, which reversed the decision. Then, in December of 1935, while America was still mired in the Great Depression, one of the New Deal's most ambitious recovery projects was argued before the highest court in the land.

The Congress shall have power . . . to declare war . . . raise and support armies . . . provide and maintain a navy . . . make rules for the government and regulation of land and naval forces . . . provide for calling forth the militia to execute the laws of the Union, suppress insurrections and repel invasions.

— Article I, Section 8, U.S. Constitution

Before the U.S. Supreme Court, the TVA claimed that the basic issue was the right of the federal government to generate and sell electricity—using its Wilson Dam near Muscle Shoals in northwest Alabama. This dam was built under the National Defense Act of 1916, during the crisis of World War I. It was designed to improve navigation on the Tennessee River and to provide electricity for nearby government-owned nitrate plants making explosives for the American war effort. At the time, proponents had justified these government operations under the war powers clause of the Constitution (see quote at left)—as well as under the commerce power (see quote, page 55).

The Congress shall have power to dispose of and make all needful rules and regulations respecting the territory or other property belonging to the United States. . . .

— Article IV, Section 3, U.S. Constitution

Now, during a peacetime crisis no less grave, supporters were suggesting that these government facilities should supply low-cost electricity, as well as nitrate for cheap fertilizer, to the 3 million people in the Tennessee Valley. The TVA told the Supreme Court that the federal operations could still be justified by the need for national preparedness. In addition, the TVA based its right to the electricity generated by the Wilson Dam on the property clause of the Constitution (see quote at left).

Ashwander and his group warned the Court against too broad an interpretation of the war, commerce, and property powers. This would pave the way, they charged, to unreasonable and unlimited government interference with the American free enterprise system. All essential businesses would be subject to possible government competition. The states would lose forever the right to control their navigable rivers and the right to allocate use of potential water power from these rivers. Ashwander's position was that government ownership and operation of the Wilson Dam and the nitrate plants was unconstitutional—and that these facilities should be sold or leased to private investors.

FOR CRITICAL THINKING

1. Would you classify this case as an interstate commerce case, a state "police powers" case, or a "balance of powers" case? Why?
2. Do you think that the war powers clause (see quote, page 58) justified the building and original operation of the Wilson Dam and the nitrate plants? If so, do you think such powers would justify continued operation at the time of the TVA case? Explain your answers.
3. Do you think that the commerce clause (see quote, page 55) applied in any way to the government's building and operation of the dam and the plants? If so, how?
4. How would you interpret in your own words Article IV, Section 3, of the Constitution (see quote, page 58)? In what way, if any, do you think it should apply to this case?
5. How do you think the Supreme Court ruled in this case?

YOUNGSTOWN SHEET & TUBE COMPANY V. SAWYER (1952)

In the spring of 1952, frustrations bloomed. The unpopular Korean War was dragging on, and American forces seemed hopelessly stalled along the 38th parallel. Savage fighting with the Chinese Communists and the North Koreans for such hill positions as "Heartbreak Ridge" and "Bloody Ridge" had proved indecisive. The situation in Korea and the fact that the Russians had tested their first atomic bomb had led President Harry S. Truman to launch a vast program to beef up the nation's strength. To him, the spring of 1952—a presidential election year—hardly appeared the right time for a nationwide steel strike. Yet that very threat loomed. And it led to an historic showdown between the President and private industry.

A minute past midnight, April 9—that was the time set for the nationwide steel strike. For months, major steel companies and the United Steelworkers union had tried to reach agreement on a new labor contract. Their long and tedious negotiations had failed.

In the last hours of April 8, President Truman stepped in. He ordered the federal government to take over the steel mills. He said that this drastic move was needed to insure an "uninterrupted supply of steel" for the defense effort, the Atomic Energy Commission, and the health of the nation's economy.

Truman's Executive Order directed his Secretary of Commerce, Charles Sawyer: (1) to seize and operate certain steel companies, (2) to dictate wages and work conditions, (3) to outline collective bargaining procedures, (4) to permit mill managements to continue their normal functions, and (5) when government control proved no longer necessary for continued steel production, to return the mills to their owners.

The seizure provoked an uproar. Mill owners, led by Youngstown Sheet & Tube Company, charged that Truman's order was unconstitutional. The government countered that it was necessary to prevent a national disaster.

Mill owners filed suit in federal district court. They demanded an order to stop the government takeover. Because of the urgency of the issue, the case rocketed to the U.S. Supreme Court in record time. Less than eight weeks elapsed between Truman's order to seize the mills and the Supreme Court's decision.

Before the high bench, Youngstown and the other steel companies charged that Truman's Executive Order amounted to lawmaking. That order, they argued, was a legislative function the Constitution had delegated to Congress—not to the President.

Government lawyers replied that the President had been acting within the framework of his constitutional powers as Chief Executive and commander-in-chief of the armed forces. They did not claim that the Constitution expressly gave him the power to seize steel mills. But they argued that, in a grave national crisis, this power should be implied from the "aggregate," or sum, of his powers under Article II of the Constitution. Specifically, they mentioned clauses providing: (1) that "the executive power shall be vested in a President"; (2) that "he shall take care that the laws shall be faithfully executed"; and (3) that he "shall be commander-in-chief of the Army and the Navy of the United States."

FOR CRITICAL THINKING

1. Would you classify this case as an interstate commerce case, a state "police powers" case, or a "balance of powers" case? Why?

2. From what authority, if any, do you think the President could order the federal government to take over and operate private businesses in a national emergency?

3. Do you agree or disagree with Youngstown's argument that the President, in seizing the mills, was "lawmaking"? If you agree, do you think he could justify this function under his powers as commander-in-chief? As Chief Executive? Give reasons for your answers.

4. Does the quotation of Justice Hugo Black (at left) help you solve this case? Explain. Do you think it is from a majority or a dissenting opinion? Why?

5. How do you think the Supreme Court ruled in this case?

In the framework of our Constitution, the President's power to see that the laws are faithfully executed refutes that he is to be a lawmaker. The Constitution limits his functions in the lawmaking process to the recommending of causes he thinks wise and the vetoing of causes he thinks bad.

— Justice Black, *Youngstown Sheet & Tube Co. v. Sawyer* (1952)

HOLTZMAN V. SCHLESINGER (1973)

In the spring of 1970, the long and bloody Vietnam War spilled its fury into neighboring Cambodia. Across the Cambodian-Vietnamese border thrust 31,000 United States and 43,000 South Vietnamese troops. Overhead screamed American jets raining American bombs. The fighting left dozens of smoking villages in the formerly neutralist country. President Richard M. Nixon announced that the strikes had been necessary to clean out North Vietnamese enemy units attacking from strongholds inside Cambodia—and endangering the planned withdrawal of American troops from South Vietnam. He said such Communist operations made the war in Southeast Asia "of one piece." Many Americans strongly disagreed. They wanted the controversial war to end, not expand.

Protests exploded on college campuses across America. At one—Kent State University—members of the National Guard fired into demonstrators, killing four students and wounding eleven. Opposition also erupted in Congress. Bills were introduced to impeach President Nixon as well as to force the end of all American involvement in Indochina. The following controversial case grew out of these heated times.

After the spring offensive, the United States withdrew its ground troops from Cambodia in June, 1970. American losses included 337 dead and 1,524 wounded. But the U.S. government claimed that the invasion had been a success—11,349 of the enemy killed, 2,328 captured, tons of weapons and supplies seized. "The only remaining American activity in Cambodia after July l," announced President Nixon, "will be air missions to [check] the movement of enemy troops and material where I find that it is necessary to protect the lives and security of our men in South Vietnam."

Many members of Congress fought to cut off even that activity. That summer Congress enacted the "Fulbright Proviso." This declared that no funds could be used for military support in Cambodia. In the winter of 1970–71, however, Congress added the following limitation to the Proviso: "Nothing contained in this section shall be construed to prohibit support of actions required to insure safe and orderly withdrawal or disengagement of United States forces from Southeast Asia, or to aid in the release of Americans held as prisoners of war." Then, in the "Special Foreign Assistance Act of 1971," members of Congress put a limit on the limitation. Congress banned the use of funds to support American ground troops in Cambodia—for any reason whatsoever.

American air strikes in Cambodia, however, continued during 1972 and 1973. And Congress stepped up its efforts to stop them. The House of Representatives—after the withdrawal of American ground troops from Vietnam and the return of American prisoners of war—refused a Nixon Administration request for $175 million to cover the costs of Cambodian bombing. Eventually, Congress passed and the President signed a resolution that read: "Notwithstanding any other provision of law, on or after

August 15, 1973, no funds herein or heretofore appropriated may be obligated or expended to finance directly or indirectly combat activities by the United States military forces in or over or from off the shores of North Vietnam, South Vietnam, Laos, or Cambodia.''

On January 27, 1973, the United States signed a peace treaty in Paris, ending American military operations in the Vietnam War. Yet American bombing of Cambodia went on. And the administration clearly meant to keep bombing until the August 15 cutoff date.

Rep. Elizabeth Holtzman, a Democratic congresswoman from New York, joined several Air Force officers serving in Asia and filed a lawsuit to shut off the Cambodia air strikes immediately. They brought suit against James R. Schlesinger, then the Acting Secretary of the Air Force. In their case in federal district court, the plaintiffs presented these principle arguments:

1. Since such military activity had not been authorized by Congress, it violated Article I, Section 8, of the Constitution, which gives Congress the power to declare war.
2. In non-emergency situations, the President cannot exercise war-making power without the ''affirmative'' consent of Congress.
3. In light of the Fulbright Proviso, Congress never approved any military activity in Cambodia once American ground troops and POW's were out of Vietnam.
4. Unless the bombing of Cambodia stopped immediately, further American pilots would be killed or captured and Cambodian civilians made homeless. ''The lives of thousands . . . will be endangered by the Executive's . . . unconstitutional conduct,'' argued the plaintiffs.

The district court, ruling in favor of Rep. Holtzman, granted an injunction banning any further American bombing in Cambodia. The defendants took their case to the U.S. Court of Appeals. Here they argued: (a) that Congress, by ordering Cambodian operations to stop on or after August 15, had indicated that bombing was authorized until that deadline date and (b) that if the Cambodian bombings were cut off before that date, vital foreign policy goals and security interests of the U.S. government would be severely injured.

The Court of Appeals, deciding in favor of the defendants, overruled the district court. The issues in the case were too important to be decided hurriedly, said the Court of Appeals. So it granted a stay of the injunction. That is, the effective date of the injunction was delayed until there could be a full hearing. And this was set for August 8.

Congresswoman Holtzman and the Air Force officers now took their appeal directly to the U.S. Supreme Court. Since the full Court was then in summer recess, they asked Justice Thurgood Marshall to cancel the Court of Appeal's stay.

"If the decision were mine alone," said Justice Marshall, "I might well conclude on the merits that continued American military operations in Cambodia are unconstitutional." But he refused on August 3 to vacate the Court of Appeals' stay. Among his reasons, he included:

1. Even though he had the power as a single justice to cancel the Court of Appeals' stay, "this power should be exercised with the greatest of caution and should be reversed for exceptional circumstances."
2. Since the Supreme Court is a body in which all the members have roughly equal authority, "its decisions reflect the views of a majority of the sitting justices." But Justice Marshall said he did not then know the views of the other justices. When one justice hears a case, he or she must act as a representative for the entire court.
3. The cutoff date, according to the congressional order, was August 15. But there were no precedents or guidelines to determine if the bombing should be halted before the deadline.

Rep. Holtzman and the other plaintiffs did not accept Justice Marshall's refusal as final. They made an appeal to a second justice, William O. Douglas, who was vacationing in the state of Washington at the time. While he said he respected the views of his fellow judge, Justice Douglas cancelled the stay and ruled on August 4 that the district court's injunction should go into effect immediately. He cited among his reasons:

1. "We live under the Constitution and in Article I, Section 8, it gives to Congress the power to 'declare war'. . . . It has become popular to think the President has that power to declare war. But there is not a word in the Constitution that grants that power to him. It runs only to Congress." In the Cambodia case, Congress had not declared war. Justice Douglas pointed out two 1863 cases in which the Supreme Court held that the President "has no power to initiate or declare a war either against a foreign nation or a domestic state . . . ."
2. Justice Douglas compared this case to a "capital case"—that is, a criminal case involving the death penalty. "The upshot is that we know that someone is about to die," he said. The Fifth Amendment (left), he pointed out, guarantees life, liberty and property. And the President cannot take life in violation of the Fifth Amendment. Besides, he reasoned, in a capital case, a decision based upon a full hearing of the facts and rights involved in the matter "follows and does not precede the stay [of execution]." In such a case, he added, "the stay is granted because death is irrevocable."

No person shall . . . be deprived of life, liberty, or property without due process of law. . . .

— 5th Amendment, U.S. Constitution (1791)

Following Justice Douglas' ruling shutting off the bombing, the defendants hurried back to Justice Marshall, seeking still another decision. And on that same day, August 4, Justice Marshall handed down a fifth and final ruling in this unusual case.

FOR CRITICAL THINKING

The Congress shall have power . . . to declare war . . . raise and support armies . . . provide and maintain a navy . . . make rules for the government and regulation of land and naval forces . . . provide for calling forth the militia to execute the laws of the Union, suppress insurrections and repel invasions.

— Article I, Section 8, U.S. Constitution

1. Would you classify this case as an interstate commerce case, a state "police powers" case, or a "balance of powers" case? Why?
2. How would you interpret in your own words all the acts of Congress in this case dealing with the U.S. military operations in Cambodia? After the resolution fixing the August 15, 1973, deadline, what was permitted and what was prohibited?
3. How would you interpret in your own words Article I, Section 8 (left)? How, if in any way, should it apply to *Holtzman v. Schlesinger*?
4. Which argument of the plaintiffs do you think is the most important? Why? Which argument of the defendant do you think is the most important? Why?
5. Which point made by Justice Marshall do you think should be given the most weight in deciding this case? Why? Which point made by Justice Douglas do you think should be given the most weight in deciding this case? Why?
6. How do you think Justice Marshall ruled in this case?

UNITED STATES V. NIXON (1974)

June 17, 1972—Presidential election year. Time: 1:52 A.M. Burglars wearing rubber gloves were rifling the files of the darkened Democratic National Headquarters in Washington's swank Watergate Office Building. A security guard making his rounds happened to notice telltale tapes on garage doors where the break-in had occurred. A police car was summoned, and within minutes, officers with guns drawn caught the burglars in the act. Seven men were arrested for trying to install electronic spying devices and steal political secrets from the Democrats. Two were identified as officials of the Republican Party's committee to re-elect President Richard Nixon; one, as a consultant to the White House itself.

Thus emerged the tip of an iceberg that would become known as the Watergate scandal. The investigation turned up reports not only of burglary, but also high-level influence peddling, disruption of the election process, and cover-up to obstruct justice. The scandal eventually would lead to the resignation of a score of top administration officials, including the President's campaign committee chairman, his finance committee chairman, and his two closest White House aides. It would reach into the Justice Department, the Federal Bureau of Investigation, the Central Intelligence Agency. It would result in the sentencing of more than a dozen persons for various crimes. It would even lead to the resignation of the President himself.

For two years after the Watergate break-in, however, the White House denied responsibility for the planning or the cover-up by either the President or any member of his staff. To establish credibility, the administration appointed a special prosecutor, who was promised complete independence to pursue the investigation before a grand jury and in the courts. In addition, the Senate Watergate Committee opened a series of nationally televised hearings probing illegal and unethical activity during the 1972 Presidential campaign. Its chairman was Sen. Sam Ervin, a Democrat of North Carolina and a recognized constitutional expert. During the investigations of 1973, the following key case arose.

Senate Watergate Committee staffers didn't realize they were nearing the pivotal moment in their investigation of the White House scandal. Behind closed doors in Room G-334 of the Senate Office Building, their questioning of Alexander P. Butterfield had dragged on all afternoon. It was 5 P.M., and Butterfield—a former aide to President Nixon who was being interviewed as a possible witness in the public committee hearings—had told them nothing particularly startling. Then one committee staff investigator, following a hunch, asked an innocent, but key question: "Are conversations in the President's office recorded?"

"I was hoping you fellows wouldn't ask me about that," replied Butterfield. Time stood still. Then the truth came tumbling out.

In 1970, said Butterfield, Nixon had ordered the Secret Service to install electronic bugs, or listening devices. Since then, all conversations had been secretly and automatically tape-recorded in the President's offices throughout the White House complex, the Lincoln Sitting Room, the Cabinet Room, and his study at Camp David. The tapes included conversations dealing not only with the Watergate scandal, but also with other governmental issues, with national security, with foreign relations, and with references to individuals.

Both the Senate Watergate Committee and the Special Prosecutor hastened to ask President Nixon to turn over the tapes. There had been serious conflict in much of the Watergate testimony. And these recordings might settle most of the disputes. As the "best evidence" of the actual conversations between the President and his aides accused of taking part in the Watergate break-in, the tapes could support or deny the testimony of many witnesses. And they could clarify the President's own role in the affair. President Nixon refused to turn over the tapes, and a long legal battle began.

In March of 1974, after numerous legal battles, the special prosecutor said the tapes were needed as evidence in the upcoming criminal trial of seven persons involved in Watergate. At that time, President Nixon was named, but not formally accused, along with the seven others in a "conspiracy" to cover up the facts about Watergate. Attacking the request for the court order, the President's lawyers made two main arguments:

(1) Conversations between a President and his advisers often deal with serious problems of state, even war and peace. They are private and should not be made public. Under the claim of "executive privilege," such conversations should not be disclosed—even to a court of law.

The claim of executive privilege was based on our constitutional system of separation of powers. That is, the makers of the Constitution divided up the basic powers of the federal government, so that each branch would serve as a check and a balance on the other. The power to make laws belongs to the legislative branch. The power to put laws into effect belongs to the executive branch. And the power to judge the laws belongs to the judicial branch. Some of the powers given to each branch are listed in the Constitution. Others are "implied" from the powers that are listed. Executive privilege, while not listed in the Constitution, is one of the implied powers of the executive branch. And this power, argued Nixon and his advisers, was total. Only the President could decide its extent and scope. Only the President, moreover, could determine when an executive communication covered by the privilege should be made known to the public. The courts had no constitutional authority to settle disputes on such matters.

(2) The federal courts had no authority to rule on a special prosecutor's demand for the tapes. The courts could only settle disputes between different branches of the government. The special prosecutor had been appointed by the U.S. Attorney General and was a member of the executive branch of the government. The President was the head of the executive branch.

In late May, 1974, the district court ruled against President Nixon. Judge John Sirica pointed out that a higher court, the U.S. Court of Appeals, had already ruled against the President's having "absolute," or total and final, executive privilege. To let the President have the final say on when to apply executive privilege, the Court of Appeals had ruled, would hurt—not support—separation of powers. The power to judge what the law is belongs to the courts, not the executive branch. Besides, said Judge Sirica, the claim of executive privilege was outweighed by the special prosecutor's need to gather evidence for use in a criminal trial.

The district court also turned down the argument that it could not settle this dispute because both the President and the special prosecutor were members of the executive branch. Judge Sirica said that the special prosecutor had been given the job by the Attorney General with the agreement of the President. And the special prosecutor had been given complete freedom to investigate the Watergate affair. That included the power to seek evidence from any source—even the President.

President Nixon appealed the case. And it eventually came before the U.S. Supreme Court.

FOR CRITICAL THINKING

1. Who appointed the U.S. Attorney General? Who appointed the special prosecutor? What were the powers and duties of the special prosecutor?
2. Under what conditions, if any, do you think a claim of executive privilege is constitutional? Does this case fall under those conditions? Explain.
3. Which do you think is more important: (a) a President's right to keep conversations with advisers private, or (b) a prosecutor's right to get evidence needed for a criminal case? Explain.
4. Should a President have a general right of executive privilege? Why? If so, do you think it should be (a) absolute or (b) limited? Explain.
5. How do you think the Supreme Court ruled in this case?

HAIG V. AGEE (1981)

The only way by which an American can lawfully leave the country or return to it is with a passport. As a travel control document, a passport is both proof of identity and proof of allegiance to the United States. In 1926 Congress passed the Passport Act, which set certain rules and regulations for passport holders. The Act, however, did not make clear which branch of government—the executive or legislative—had the power to revoke a passport. The question of whether the President could withhold a passport for national security reasons arose in the following case.

It was a hot summer day in 1974 on the Caribbean island of Jamaica. Suddenly the sound of gunfire rang out, as bullets strafed the home of an American resident, Richard Kinsman. Just four days earlier, Kinsman had been identified as the Jamaica station-chief of the U.S. Central Intelligence Agency. Now his life was in danger.

Kinsman's identify had been disclosed by a fellow American, Philip Agee. Agee himself had been a CIA member, spending nine years in the secret organization before resigning in protest in 1969. He then vowed "to fight the United States CIA wherever it is operating."

Over the years Agee did just that, traveling from country to country, exposing the names of local undercover agents. He also wrote a best-selling book called *Inside the Company: A CIA Diary.* In his book he revealed the names of hundreds of CIA agents working abroad. Two such American agents, posing as agricultural workers in El Salvador, were later murdered.

In 1979, in the midst of the Iranian hostage crisis, Secretary of State Cyrus Vance ordered the revocation of Agee's passport. Agee had proposed that the crisis be resolved by exchanging CIA files on Iran for the American hostages. The furious Vance acted under regulations issued by the State Department in 1966 that authorized withholding a passport when "the Secretary determines that [an individual's] activities abroad are causing or are likely to cause serious damage to the national security or the foreign policy of the United States." The State Department said that Agee could return home, but would no longer be able to use an American passport to travel to other countries.

Agee immediately filed suit. He said that the President, acting through the Secretary of State, had no power to take away his passport. Only Congress, he claimed, could do so. Agee also said that the Secretary of State's decision violated his First Amendment right to criticize government policies.

The government countered by citing past instances where the executive branch had withheld passports. It said, furthermore, that while the Passport Act of 1926 did not authorize the Secretary of State to revoke a passport, neither did it specify that the Secretary could *not* do so. Agee had clearly created serious problems for American foreign relations and foreign policy. The only avenue open to the government to limit his activities was to restrict his foreign travel.

As for Agee's claim that his First Amendment rights were being violated, the government argued that he was perfectly free to criticize American policy—but from now on he could only do so at home.

Two lower courts agreed with Agee, holding that Congress had never specifically authorized the State Department to revoke a passport on national security grounds. Agee's passport was returned. The new Secretary of State, Alexander Haig, then took the case to the Supreme Court in 1981.

FOR CRITICAL THINKING

1. Should the federal government have the power to prevent a citizen's travels because it disapproves of his or her views? If so, explain under what circumstances. If not, explain why not.

2. Do you agree with the government's argument that Agee was a threat to national security? Why or why not?

3. Why did the government choose to revoke Agee's passport? How could such an action have hurt him?

4. Which branch of government should have the authority to revoke a passport—the executive or the legislative? Why?

5. Does the quote from Chief Justice Burger (at left) help you decide this case? Explain.

6. How do you think the Supreme Court ruled in this case?

The history of passport controls since the earliest days of the republic shows congressional recognition of executive authority to withhold passports on the basis of substantial reasons of national security and foreign policy.

— Chief Justice Burger, *Haig v. Agee* (1981)

EXPLORING THE MAIN IDEAS

WHAT DO YOU THINK?

1. What case or cases in this chapter, if any, involved the commerce clause? Which involved the elastic clause? Which involved the war clause? Which involved the property clause? Which involved the police powers?

2. From what you have read in this chapter, during what periods did the federal government tend to enlarge its powers? Why? Support your answer with examples and causes.
3. At what points, if any, in this chapter did you detect a decided change in the values and views underlying Supreme Court decisions? Explain.
4. Which of the cases in this chapter do you regard as the wisest determination of national policy by the Supreme Court? Which do you regard as least wise? Which do you think would have the greatest impact on the problems confronting America today? Explain your answers fully.

THINGS TO DO

1. Make a poster showing several of the following constitutional powers: the commerce clause, the elastic clause, the war clause, the property clause, the police powers. With each type of power, include: (a) the language of the clause from which the power stems, (b) a newspaper clipping giving a modern example of the power, and (c) an illustration clipped from a newspaper or magazine symbolizing the power.
2. Write a short dramatic play involving a fictionalized President of the United States faced with constitutional issues similar to those that confronted President Harry S. Truman in the *Youngstown* case.
3. Using the procedures outlined at the back of this book, conduct a mock trial of the *Holtzman v. Schlesinger* case.

Illustration Review

Now that you have finished this chapter's cases, re-analyze the pictures on pages 46–47. Which cases relate to which pictures? In what ways, if any, would your answers to the questions in "Illustration Analysis" at the beginning of the chapter now change? In what ways, if any, would your answers remain the same?

DEMOCRATS
FOR THE RIGHT
DEMOCRATIC PARTY
OFFICIAL
PRIMARY ELECTION BALLOT
MAY 3, 1966
DEMOCRATIC PARTY
WILCOX COUNTY
Instructions: To vote for any candidate make a cross (X) in the square in the appropriate column, according to your choice.
For United States Senator—Vote for One
JOHN G. CROMMELIN
FRANK E. DIXON
JOHN SPARKMAN
MRS. FRANK R. STEWART
For Governor—Vote for One
JOHN PATTERSON
SHERMAN BLACKSTONE POWELL
A. W. TODD
MRS. GEORGE C. WALLACE
CHARLES WOODS
CARL ELLIOTT
RICHMOND M. FLOWERS
JAMES E. (Big Jim) FOLSOM
BOB GILCHRIST
(MR.) EUNICE I. GORE
For Lieutenant Governor—Vote for One
ALBERT BREWER
NEIL METCALF
JOHN A. REYNOLDS
JOHN M. TYSON
For Representative in Congress From the First Congressional District—Vote for One
WILL D. BAAS
RICHARD E. McPHEARSON
WARREN L. FINCH
For State Senator Nineteenth Senatorial District—Vote for One
ROLAND COOPER
MASTON M. MIMS
LONNIE L. BROWN
For Member of the House of Representatives Thirty-Fourth District, Place No. 1—Vote for One
J. THOMAS JONES
THOMAS N. STALLWORTH
W. E. (Gene) GARRETT
For Member of the House of Representatives Thirty-Fourth District, Place No. 2—Vote for One
WM. D. (Billy) MELTON
WILEY SALTER
WILLIAM L. (Bill) CHAPPELL
For Sheriff—Vote for One
WALTER J. CALHOUN
P. C. JENKINS
TO BE SOLD, BY PUBLIC AUCTION,

4 Slavery, Citizenship, and the Vote

In 1846 when Dred Scott—a frail and unskilled slave—signed legal papers to gain his freedom, little did he realize that he would become a historic figure in a national controversy. Little did he realize that his humble lawsuit, dragged out for a decade, would so divide the United States that it spurred on the forces plummeting Americans toward a long and bloody civil war.

A background file, had any ever been kept for this tragic figure, would have provided a capsule view of a slave's unsettled life. *Name:* Dred Scott. *Born:* Southampton County, Virginia, approximately 1795, to slave parents, the property of Capt. Peter Blow. *1827:* Capt. Blow moves to St. Louis with his family, slaves, and other property. *1831:* Blow dies, his daughter, Elizabeth Blow, becomes the owner of Dred Scott. *1833:* Elizabeth Blow sells Scott to Dr. John A. Emerson, a surgeon in the Army. *1834:* Emerson, transferred to Rock Island, Illinois, takes Scott along as a servant. *1837:* Emerson, transferred again, takes Scott to Fort Snelling, near modern-day Minneapolis. *1838:* Emerson and Scott return to St. Louis.

The journeys with Emerson laid the grounds for Dred Scott's lawsuit. The issue: Was a slave made free by residing in a state or territory where slavery was banned? The first Emerson-Scott journey was from Missouri, a state where slavery was permitted, to Illinois, a state where slavery was prohibited. The second journey was to Fort Snelling—which lay in that part of the Louisiana Territory where slavery had been banned by act of Congress. The Missouri Compromise of 1820 had declared that the territory north of 36°30′ was "free soil."

The judicial power [of the federal court system] shall extend to all cases, in law and equity, arising under this Constitution, the laws of the United States, and treaties made, or which shall be made, under their authority . . . to controversies between citizens of different states. . . .

— Article III, Section 2, Clause 1, U.S. Constitution

When Dr. Emerson died, Dred Scott was left to the widow, Mrs. Irene Sanford Emerson. In the mid-1840's, she moved to New York, leaving Scott in St. Louis. Here he was left in the charge of his original owner's two wealthy sons, Henry and Taylor Blow. Henry, a lawyer and head of a railroad, was also active in the antislavery political movement. He helped finance the lawsuit asking Missouri courts to declare Dred Scott a free man. The case title: "Scott, a Man of Color v. Emerson." Irene Sanford Emerson was technically the defendant. But she was not proslavery. And like the Blows, she mainly wanted a court ruling that would settle the legal status of a slave who lived on "free soil."

Scott won his freedom in one of Missouri's lower courts. But the state's supreme court overturned this decision and affirmed Scott's status as a slave. Undaunted by this setback, Dred Scott's antislavery friends encouraged him to take his case to the federal courts. Article III, Section 2, of the Constitution gives the federal courts jurisdiction in disputes between the citizens of different states. Scott's supporters arranged a phony sale of the slave to John Sanford, Irene Sanford Emerson's brother. Having done this, they contended that Scott, a resident of Missouri, could sue Sanford, a resident of New York, in federal court.

A federal court in Missouri agreed to hear Scott's suit for his freedom and thereby recognized his right as a citizen of Missouri to sue a citizen of New York. The jury in the case, however, decided in favor of Sanford. Scott then appealed to the U.S. Supreme Court.

In 1857, the Supreme Court ruled against Dred Scott. A majority declared that under Missouri law, which controlled

Scott's status, he was still a slave and not a citizen of the United States. Therefore, held the majority, Scott did not have the right to sue in the federal courts under the pretense that he was a citizen. The Court could have stopped right there. But its decision grew far more complicated.

Originally, seven justices had intended to dismiss the case simply for lack of federal jurisdiction—that is, authority to decide the case. However, they learned that two dissenting justices intended to write opinions, affirming the power of Congress in the Missouri Compromise to outlaw slavery in United States territories. So the majority justices wrote separate opinions, denying that Congress possessed such power. The result was a jumble of nine separate and often conflicting opinions.

Despite the fact that there were nine opinions, the one written by Chief Justice Roger B. Taney was the most influential at the time and came to be the most widely quoted ever since. It denied that Dred Scott or any other man of African descent could be considered a citizen of the United States or of the state of Missouri in the sense that the word "citizen" was used in the Constitution. Taney stated that the framers of the Constitution did not think of blacks as part of the "sovereign people" who formed the government of the United States. The Chief Justice went on to say that blacks were "at that time considered as a subordinate and inferior class of beings." He said that slaves "had no rights or privileges but such as those who held the power and the government might choose to grant them." Only two other justices agreed with Taney on this extreme position.

The Chief Justice next turned to the question of whether Dred Scott had been set free by his residence in Illinois or at Fort Snelling. He declared that Congress had no power to ban slavery in the territories of the United States. Therefore the Missouri Compromise's attempt to impose such a ban was unconstitutional. Any attempt in the territories to deprive owners of their property rights in slaves was, according to Taney, a clear violation of the Fifth Amendment's guarantee of "due process" (see quote at left). Taney said, "An act of Congress which deprives a citizen of his liberty or property, without due process of law, merely because he came himself or brought his property into a particular territory of the United States, and who had committed no offense against the laws, could hardly be dignified with the name of due process of law." Taney concluded that, since Congress had had no power to prohibit slavery in the territory, "neither Dred Scott himself, nor any of his family, were made free by being carried into this territory."

No person shall . . . be deprived of life, liberty, or property, without due process of law.

— 5th Amendment, U.S. Constitution (1791)

Public reaction was stormy. The decision, which many had hoped would settle the overheated slavery issue, settled practically nothing. North and South headed even more relentlessly down the road to war.

Meanwhile, Dred Scott's owners were disappointed because they had failed to get a politically favorable ruling. A few weeks after the Supreme Court decision, they set him free. During the next year, Dred Scott worked as a porter at Barnum's Hotel in St. Louis. Then, on September 17, 1858, he died of tuberculosis. Henry Blow paid the funeral expenses.

IN YOUR OPINION

1. Do you agree or disagree with Chief Justice Taney that, under our original Constitution, slaves were not citizens and had "no rights or privileges" except those granted them by the people in power. Explain.
2. Do you agree or disagree with Taney that the Missouri Compromise of 1820 deprived slave owners in "free soil" territory of their property without "due process of law"? Explain.
3. Do you think this was a just or an unjust decision? Why? If you had decided this case, considering all the problems of the era, how would you rule? Why?
4. Do you think that the basic rights of citizenship should ever be suspended for any reason? If so, during what periods? For what reasons?
5. How much control do you think the Constitution and federal laws have over state elections? How much control should be left to state laws? Explain.

Illustration Analysis

Analyze the pictures on pages 70–71. Why do you think the design overlaps the slave poster and the face of Liberty? Which seems to prevail—slavery or liberty? What is symbolized by the photo of the hands and the ballot? In what way does this photo relate to citizenship?

PAINFUL PATH TO FULL CITIZENSHIP

The *Dred Scott* case, constitutional experts have said, was a "public calamity." Never had there been such widespread outrage over a Supreme Court decision. Republicans believed the very existence of their young party was threatened. Their chief principle, "free soil" in the territories, had been ruled unconstitutional. Whereas ardent proslavery Democrats in the South were jubilant, Northern Democrats were dismayed. They felt that the decision seriously jeopardized their compromise principle of "popular sovereignty"—allowing the settlers of a territory to decide whether it would be organized as slave or free.

The badly split wings of the Democratic Party could not agree on a presidential candidate for the election of 1860. Republican Abraham Lincoln, man of the hour, swept into the White House. Southern states, fearing for the future of their plantation and slave economy, seceded. And the Civil War, the bloodiest in American history, erupted.

ORIGINS OF THE "PECULIAR INSTITUTION"

Slavery, that explosive problem Southerners liked to call their "peculiar institution," began in America in the seventeenth century. In 1619, the first Africans arrived in Virginia—as indentured servants, however, and not as slaves. Originally, their contracts of indenture were the same as for whites. Freedom was earned by serving, for five or seven years, the person who had paid the servant's passage to the Americas. By mid-century, however, blacks imported by the colonies received no contracts of indenture. They were no longer servants; they were slaves. They had no rights at all. Their legal status: chattel—personal property.

After the American Revolution, leaders in both the North and the South began to feel uneasy about slavery. It didn't seem in harmony with the ideals of liberty on which the new republic had been founded. On their own, most Northern states abolished slavery. Their smaller farms did not require the large-scale cheap labor upon which the Southern plantation system increasingly depended—especially after it developed, with the help of the cotton gin, into a one-crop economy.

SLAVERY AND THE CONSTITUTION

The word "slavery" appeared nowhere in the Constitution of 1787. It was a delicate issue. Indeed, in only three passages was the subject even alluded to. And these were attempted compromises between Northern and Southern interests. Article I, Section 2, Clause 3, said that, in determining the number of congressional representations for each state as well as its tax burden, only "three-fifths of all other persons" (i.e., slaves) should be counted. Article I, Section 9, Clause 1, barred Congress from stopping the "migration or importation of such persons" (i.e., foreign slave trade) before 1808. And Article IV, Section 2, Clause 3, required any "person held in service or labor" (i.e., slave) who ran away to a free state to be returned to his or her owner. The Constitution, then, where it mentioned the subject of slavery at all, avoided any mention by name.

On rights and on citizenship for blacks, the Constitution was silent. The Supreme Court, in the *Dred Scott* case, interjected its own doctrines on these points.

POST-CIVIL WAR AMENDMENTS

Neither slavery nor involuntary servitude, except as a punishment for a crime whereof the party shall have been duly convicted, shall exist within the United States, or any place subject to their jurisdiction.

— 13th Amendment, U.S. Constitution (1865)

The doctrines of the *Dred Scott* case were set aside, however, by the three post-Civil War amendments—the first formal changes in the Constitution in a half-century. The Thirteenth Amendment (1865) outlawed slavery and badges of slavery. The Fourteenth Amendment (1868) helped define citizenship, national and state; it also barred a state from violating a citizen's rights to "due process of law" and "equal protection of the laws." The Fifteenth Amendment (1870) pledged the United States government to see that none of its citizens were denied the right to vote because of "race, color, or previous condition of servitude."

Only in the most general terms did the Fourteenth Amendment define citizenship. The Supreme Court, interpreting the privileges and immunities clause through the years, has fleshed

All persons born or naturalized in the United States, and subject to the jurisdiction thereof, are citizens of the United States and of the state wherein they reside. No state shall make or enforce any law which shall abridge the privileges or immunities of citizens of the United States; nor shall any state deprive any person of life, liberty, or property, without due process of law, nor deny to any person within its jurisdiction the equal protection of the laws.

— 14th Amendment, U.S. Constitution (1868)

out that definition a bit. Citizenship involves certain basic rights and duties. United States citizens have the right to assemble—and to approach their government. They can pass freely from state to state, carry on interstate commerce, use the nation's navigable streams and rivers. They have the right to vote for national officials and have the privilege of the writ of habeas corpus.

SUFFRAGE: THE FUNDAMENTAL RIGHT

The most fundamental right of citizenship, however, is the right to vote. Ironically, suffrage has been restricted in America throughout much of its history. Only free, adult, male property-owners could vote during the colonial period. In many colonies, voters also had to belong to the established church. After the Revolution, the new states gradually abolished the property and religious restrictions.

The Constitution left to the states the general authority to determine who could vote. That was true for federal as well as state elections. Congress was given little control over voting. It could only regulate the "time, place, and manner" of holding federal elections.

On the other side of the scale, for the balancing duties of citizenship, the Supreme Court has looked to certain federal laws. Interpreting these, the Court has said that American citizens must bear "full faith and allegiance" to the United States. They must support and defend the Constitution and federal laws against all enemies.

CITIZENSHIP ACQUIRED

The right of citizens of the United States to vote shall not be denied or abridged by the United States or by any state on account of race, color, or previous condition of servitude.

— 15th Amendment, U.S. Constitution (1870)

This basic bond of rights and duties called "citizenship"—how does a person acquire it? According to the Fourteenth Amendment, United States citizenship is acquired in three ways. First, a person may be "born" to it: born in this country, as well as born to American parents on foreign soil. Second, an alien immigrant may be voluntarily "naturalized" under a process outlined by federal laws. And third, persons "subject to the jurisdiction" of the United States, such as American Indians and residents of certain dependencies, may have citizenship thrust upon them.

CITIZENSHIP LOST

Citizenship is man's basic right for it is nothing less than the right to have rights.

— Chief Justice Warren, *Perez v. Brownell* (1958)

The bond of allegiance to one's native country—the basic duty of citizenship—is unbreakable—or so held an ancient English tradition. A few early American cases agreed. But, since a congressional statute of 1868, the United States has recognized the right to voluntarily give up one's citizenship.

Whether the government may ever take away an American's citizenship has been roundly debated. In the Nationality Act of 1940, Congress outlined certain actions for which the federal

Citizenship is not a license that expires on misbehavior.

— Chief Justice Warren, *Trop v. Dulles* (1958)

government could revoke citizenship. These included: (a) leaving the country to escape the draft, (b) desertion from military service during wartime, and (c) voting in a foreign election. In a series of subsequent cases, however, the Supreme Court knocked down each one of these provisions. In *Afroyim v. Rusk* (1967), the Court held that the government cannot revoke a person's citizenship against his or her will for any reason. If the bond is to be broken, one must voluntarily break it.

EX PARTE MERRYMAN (1861)

War—by nature, it threatens liberties, customs, ways of life. Typically, these are lost by the vanquished. But in a desperate struggle for survival, the victors may also find that they have forfeited some of their liberties. In the Civil War, emotions and hatreds became so feverish that the calm reason needed to analyze weighty constitutional issues was all but impossible. President Lincoln and his government assumed unprecedented powers. Military authorities began trying civilians. In this atmosphere, the following case occurred.

Baltimore in 1861 was a city with a divided soul. The Civil War was in its first days, and tensions ran high. Washington, D.C., the nation's capital fifty miles to the south, sat threatened on all sides. Virginia to the south and west had already seceded from the Union. And many feared that Baltimore's own state of Maryland, located to the north and east of Washington, would follow Virginia's example.

As Union troops passed through Baltimore on their way to defend Washington, Confederate sympathizers attacked. Some troops were killed. Others were wounded. Among the Maryland secessionists suspected of the attacks was John Merryman. Union forces said the prominent Baltimorean not only had organized the attacks but also had stolen arms from a federal arsenal.

At 2:00 A.M. on May 25, 1861, John Merryman was hauled from his bed and placed under arrest by a band of soldiers from Pennsylvania. He was imprisoned at historic Fort McHenry, overlooking Baltimore harbor, where "The Star-Spangled Banner" had flown during the bombardment by British warships in the War of 1812. Now, the fort's garrison was under the command of Union General George Cadwalader.

Allowed to see a lawyer, Merryman petitioned for a writ of habeas corpus—that is, a court order requiring a prisoner to be brought before a judge to determine whether he or she is being legally held. Merryman's petition was presented to the Chief Justice of the U.S. Supreme Court, Roger B. Taney. Since no charges had been made, and no grounds shown for Merryman's arrest and imprisonment, Taney granted the writ. He did so in his capacity as a judge for the federal circuit court of Baltimore.

Taney's writ ordered General Cadwalader to bring Merryman before the federal court in Baltimore at 11:00 A.M. on May 27.

Neither the general nor his prisoner appeared. Instead, a military aide strode into the court and read a letter from General Cadwalader. This letter said that Cadwalader had been authorized by President Lincoln to suspend the writ of habeas corpus and, therefore, that he would not deliver John Merryman to the court.

Furious, Chief Justice Taney ruled Cadwalader in contempt of court. He ordered that the general be taken into custody and brought into court the following day, May 28.

The atmosphere in Baltimore was explosive as people awaited the outcome of this confrontation between the Chief Justice and an army general. Many realized that the showdown was ultimately between the Chief Justice of the Supreme Court and the President of the United States. Some feared that Taney himself would be arrested by the military. Perhaps he too would be imprisoned in Fort McHenry. As the 83-year-old Chief Justice, bent with illness, hobbled to the courthouse on May 28, a crowd of respectful spectators watched in silence. Finally, at noon, the Chief Justice called upon a United States marshal to deliver Cadwalader before the court. Few were surprised to discover that the general had not been taken into custody. The marshal explained that he had gone to Fort McHenry but had been refused entrance.

Clearly, General Cadwalader had no intention of heeding Taney's orders. The Chief Justice reminded the marshal that he had the power to raise a posse to seize General Cadwalader. However, since it would have been impossible to overcome the garrison, Taney excused the marshal from any further responsibility in the matter. The Chief Justice then delivered a verbal opinion in *Ex parte Merryman.* Later, he put it into writing.

FOR CRITICAL THINKING

1. Why was John Merryman arrested? Explain.
2. Do you think the army had the power to arrest Merryman?
3. Why did John Merryman think he should be released on a writ of habeas corpus? Explain.
4. Was Merryman a citizen of the United States? What difference, if any, should that make in this case?
5. Does the quote from the Constitution at left help you decide this case? This clause falls in Article I, which deals with "The Legislative Department." What effect, if any, should that have on this case? Why?
6. How do you think the Supreme Court ruled in this case?

The privilege of the writ of habeas corpus shall not be suspended, unless when in cases of rebellion or invasion the public safety may require it.

— Article I, Section 9, Clause 2, U.S. Constitution

KOREMATSU V. UNITED STATES (1944)

In the emergency of wartime, American government and military authorities have typically received—or taken—greater power over civilians. Government has often assumed, for example, increased control over private property. Dealing with civilians suspected of disloyalty has also provoked critical problems. Citizens have experienced at least a temporary loss of liberties they customarily practice in peacetime. When such restrictions were applied to all Americans, it was one thing. When they were applied, as in the following case, to a special class of citizens, it produced a constitutional challenge that is bitterly recalled to this day.

December 7, 1941: Japan's surprise air attack on Pearl Harbor, Hawaii, destroyed or damaged much of the United States Pacific Fleet. More than 2,300 Americans were killed; the nation was shocked and frightened. As Congress declared war on Japan the following day, Americans began scrambling to defend themselves.

Stunned by a string of early Japanese victories in the South Pacific, Americans feared that their own West Coast might be invaded. Many believed that in preparation for such an assault the country would be rocked by espionage and sabotage.

Prejudice against Japanese people grew rampant in America. On the West Coast, discrimination against Chinese and Japanese had long been practiced. Now, during the war crisis of early 1942, many turned their wrath on the 112,000 people of Japanese descent living in the region. More than 70,000 were United States citizens. The rest were resident aliens. There had never been a single case of espionage or sabotage by an American of Japanese descent. But many now feared there might be.

As protection against spies and saboteurs, President Franklin D. Roosevelt signed Executive Order No. 9066 on February 19. It gave certain military commanders the power to define areas from which they could exclude any or all persons. Congress ratified the President's order on March 21, when it passed a law that ordered military authorities to remove from the coast all Japanese Americans—citizens as well as aliens.

Loyalty is a matter of mind and of heart, not of race. That indeed is the history of America.

— Justice Douglas, *Hirabayashi v. United States* (1943)

Three days after Congress had passed the law, General John L. De Witt, commander of the Western Defense Command, established a curfew for all people of Japanese ancestry, citizens and aliens alike. It required them to remain in their homes from 8:00 P.M. to 6:00 A.M. A few days after that, General De Witt ordered all people of Japanese descent to remain in a West Coast military area until further notice.

Then, on May 3, De Witt announced Civilian Exclusion Order No. 34. This ordered all Japanese Americans, whether aliens or citizens, to leave the military area. No question of loyalty to the United States was raised. The Japanese Americans were forced to report to assembly centers, from which they were transported to so-called "relocation centers" in the interior.

Trapped in the web of these events was Fred Toyosoburo Korematsu. Of Japanese ancestry, he was born in Oakland, California. A graduate of Oakland High School, he had tried twice to enlist in the army. But he was turned down for a physical disability. Before and after Pearl Harbor, he worked in defense plants in the San Francisco area. When the exclusion order was announced, Fred Korematsu was in his early twenties. Had he obeyed the order, he would have been separated from his girl friend, who was Caucasian. Rather than submit to confinement in the assembly and relocation centers, he ran away. Posing as Chinese, he took a job in a trailer park.

The young citizen's bolt for freedom was in vain. Arrested before the end of May, Korematsu was tried in a federal district court. The verdict: guilty of knowingly violating Civilian Exclusion Order No. 34. Next, he appealed to the U.S. Circuit Court of Appeals. His conviction sustained, Korematsu was confined in a "relocation center" in Topaz, Utah. Finally, in October, 1944, the U.S. Supreme Court heard a review of the case in *Korematsu v. United States.*

Before the high court, Korematsu argued that Executive Order No. 9066 and the Act of Congress of March 21, 1942, were unconstitutional. He said they exceeded the war powers of both the President and Congress. He charged that the March 21 statute was an unconstitutional delegation by Congress of its legislative powers. In addition, Korematsu contended that Civilian Exclusion Order No. 34 was an exercise of illegally delegated legislative powers and that it discriminated against Japanese Americans solely on the basis of race. By May of 1942, he said, there was no longer any real danger of a Japanese invasion on the West Coast. And the exclusion of people of Japanese descent from the region appeared to be a form of class punishment reflecting the hostility of some Americans.

The federal government argued that the only issue in the case was Korematsu's violation of Civilian Exclusion Order No. 34. The decree, said the government, was justified as an emergency action under the war powers of the President and Congress. Korematsu had knowingly violated the exclusion order. Therefore, his conviction should be affirmed.

FOR CRITICAL THINKING

Korematsu was not excluded from the military area because of hostility to him or his race. He was excluded because we are at war with the Japanese Empire, because the . . . authorities feared an invasion of our West Coast and felt constrained to take proper security measures. . . .

— Justice Black, *Korematsu v. United States* (1944)

1. How do you interpret in your own words the act passed by Congress on March 21, 1942?
2. Was it reasonable for United States authorities to believe that Japan might invade the West Coast in January, 1942? Was it more reasonable or less reasonable for these officials to expect an invasion in May, 1942? Explain your answers.
3. Did American fears of invasion, espionage, and sabotage justify the exclusion of people of Japanese ancestry from the West Coast? Why?
4. Since America was at war with Japan, Germany, and Italy and since the U.S. Government excluded people of Japanese descent from the West Coast, why do you think the government did not exclude people of German and Italian descent from the East Coast?

This [is] legalization of racism. Racial discrimination in any form and in any degree has no justifiable part whatever in our democratic way of life. It is unattractive in any setting, but it is utterly revolting among a free people who have embraced the principles set forth in the Constitution of the United States.

— Justice Murphy, *Korematsu v. United States* (1944)

5. Do you think that Japanese Americans posed more of a security threat to the United States than German Americans or Italian Americans? Why or why not?

6. Was there any charge that Fred Korematsu was disloyal or that he personally posed a security threat to the United States? What effect should the question of Korematsu's loyalty have on the outcome of his case? Why?

7. Do the quotes from Justice Black (page 80) and from Justice Murphy (at left) help you decide this case? Explain. Which do you think is from the majority opinion? Which from a dissent? Explain.

8. Which, if any, of Korematsu's civil rights were violated by Exclusion Order No. 34? Explain your answer.

9. How do you think the Supreme Court ruled in this case?

BAKER V. CARR (1962)

A thorny issue of suffrage that has long plagued American democracy has been: How much should each vote count? The problem was aggravated by rural voters in numerous states becoming over-represented and urban voters, under-represented. An elected representative from a rural district often represented far fewer voters than his or her counterpart in an urban district. In the rural district, therefore, each person's vote counted more than in the urban district. Should this be a matter for each state to settle by its legislature or voters? Or should courts intervene?

In Colegrove v. Green *(1946), the Supreme Court, in effect, had ruled "yes" to the first question and "no" to the second. Under-represented voters in Illinois, complaining that voting districts were unequal, asked for a court order stopping the state from holding an election using these districts. The Court refused to intervene, saying that this was a "political" issue. The controversial subject came up again in the following case.*

Urban voters in Tennessee were bitter. Since 1901, the state legislature had passed no new law apportioning the number of legislators for each voting district. In over a half-century, there had been vast shifts in population from farms to towns and cities. As a result, by 1960, districts for the house of representatives ranged in population from 3,454 to 79,301—a ratio of 23 to 1. Thus the 3,454 rural residents with their elected representative had 23 times as much power in the state legislature as the 79,301 urban residents with their single representative. State senate districts in 1960 ranged from 39,727 residents to 237,905 residents—a ratio of 6 to 1. Urban voters felt unjustly under-represented. They complained that urgent problems of the cities were being ignored by the legislature.

A provision in the Tennessee constitution called for a reapportionment—that is, a new distribution of the number of legislators on the basis of population—every ten years. But rural politicians, who held the balance of power in the legislature, had consistently refused to join in any measures that would result in reapportionment.

Frustrated in their efforts to get the state legislature to reapportion itself, a group of urban voters took their case to a federal district court. Led by Mayor Charles W. Baker of Nashville, they filed a lawsuit against the Tennessee Secretary of State, Joe C. Carr. The plaintiffs complained that their voting rights had been watered down by the state legislature's refusal to reapportion itself. They had thus been denied "equal protection of the laws" guaranteed by the Fourteenth Amendment (see quote at left).

No state shall . . . deny to any person within its jurisdiction the equal protection of the laws.

— 14th Amendment, U.S. Constitution (1868)

In dismissing this case, the federal court said that it lacked jurisdiction over the subject matter. It thus indicated that legislative apportionment was a political issue not for the courts, but for the legislature—and ultimately the voters—to decide. The district court admitted that "the legislature of Tennessee is guilty of a clear violation of the state constitution and of the rights of the plaintiffs" and that "the evil is a serious one which should be corrected without further delay." But, citing the precedent of *Colegrove v. Green* (1946), the court said it could not act.

The plaintiffs appealed to the U.S. Supreme Court. Their case was argued before the high court in April and again in October of 1961. Here they argued that their civil rights were violated by the Tennessee statute of 1901. This was done, they said, by the unjust system of apportionment perpetuated by this law. As a result, plaintiffs had been denied the "equal protection of the laws." Before the Supreme Court they continued their quest for an injunction to stop the state from holding further elections under the 1901 statute—plus an order directing either (a) a strict mathematical reapportionment of voting districts, or (b) at large elections—for the state as a whole, without voting districts.

The U.S. Department of Justice filed an argument in this case on the side of the plaintiff as *amicus curiae,* or "a friend of the court." Speaking for the executive branch of the federal government, the department declared that many states had done nothing to improve apportionment for 25 to 50 years. "The only realistic remedy," federal lawyers said, "is federal judicial action." A number of states had shown that they had no intention of reapportioning their legislative districts. As a result, many urban areas were grossly under-represented in their state legislatures.

In defense of his state, Secretary of State Carr argued that the issue of legislative apportionment was "political" in nature. Therefore, it was a "nonjusticiable" issue for the federal courts. In other words, the federal courts had no right to interfere in the state's political arguments.

FOR CRITICAL THINKING

1. Why did Mayor Baker go to the federal courts to request that the state legislature be reapportioned? Explain your answer.

2. What were the results of the over-representation of rural areas and the under-representation of urban areas in the Tennessee legislature?
3. Do you think that reapportionment is a "political" question that ought to be left to the state legislature to decide? Explain.
4. What effect, if any, do you think the equal protection clause of the Fourteenth Amendment (quoted on page 82) should have on this case? Explain.
5. Does Article III, Section 2, of the Constitution (quoted at left) help you decide this case? Explain.
6. How do you think the Supreme Court ruled in this case?

> The judicial power shall extend to all cases, in law and equity, arising under this Constitution, the laws of the United States, and treaties made, or which shall be made, under their authority. . . .
>
> — Article III, Section 2, Clause 1, U.S. Constitution

OREGON V. MITCHELL (1970)

Women leaders campaigned vigorously for the Fifteenth Amendment (1870) to help win the vote for black men. They also sought to have the amendment apply to females as well. But the move failed. Frustrated, but more determined than ever, women civic leaders pressed their drives for suffrage. In Minor v. Happersett *(1875), the Supreme Court dealt the suffragists a setback. The privileges and immunities clause, said the Court, did not make unconstitutional a Missouri law excluding women from voting. The Constitution had left each state to decide which of its citizens could vote. And states had traditionally excluded women. (In 1920, the Nineteenth Amendment in effect, nullified the* Minor *case by granting American women their hard-earned suffrage.) In the following case, the Supreme Court was asked to extend the vote to another huge segment of the population—young Americans between the ages of 18 and 21.*

Three reforms in the Voting Rights Act passed by Congress during 1970 provoked a furor among states across the land—and spawned a host of lawsuits. One provision involved a ban on literacy tests for voter registration; another, a ban on residency requirements. But most of the attention swirled about a controversial new feature to lower the voting age in both national and state elections from 21 to 18.

The immediate impact promised to be sweeping. U.S. Census Bureau projections indicated that, initially, 11.5 million young Americans would be given the vote—including 4.1 million workers, 4 million college students, 1 million housewives, 900,000 high school students, and 800,000 military personnel.

Most of the wrath thundered from the states. Many argued that Congress had usurped the powers of the states by setting election regulations and voter qualifications. Others contended that, to lower the voting age as well as to ban literacy tests and residency requirements, a constitutional amendment ought to have been used—instead of an act of Congress.

Both proponents and opponents were eager to have courts settle the constitutionality of the reforms as quickly as possible. Consequently, they brought suits against each other. Oregon and

Texas sued the federal government—in the name of U.S. Attorney General John Mitchell. The two states sought a court order that would prevent him from enforcing the 18-year-old vote provision. At the same time the federal government sued two states, Arizona and Idaho. The government asked the court to stop the states from enforcing their laws to the extent that these conflicted with the 18-year-old vote and the bans on literacy tests and residence requirements. Since a state was a party in each of the suits, all four suits were taken directly to the Supreme Court. Because of Article III, Section 2, of the Constitution (see quote, page 83), it was the court of "original jurisdiction" with authority to initially try each of the suits and to decide the facts as well as the law.

Evidence introduced in the Supreme Court detailed the 1970 voting provision passed by Congress. First, states were prohibited for five years from using any literacy tests to decide whether a person could register to vote. Such tests—typically based upon a registrant's ability to read and write, and to understand certain constitutional provisions—had long been used by Southern state officials to eliminate blacks from voting. Second, the 1970 provisions barred states in an election for President or Vice President from disqualifying any voters because they had failed to reside in the state for a given minimum period. And third, the 1970 statute lowered to 18 the minimum age for voting in all federal, state, and local elections.

The 1970 provisions also extended the Voting Rights Act of 1965, which had been due to expire after five years. That statute—passed by Congress to insure the voting rights of blacks and other minorities—had banned literacy tests and provided for federal registration of voters.

Before the Supreme Court, Oregon, Texas, Arizona, and Idaho argued that the Constitution gives states the power to regulate elections and to determine voter qualifications. The four states cited Article I, Section 4, of the Constitution, which declared: "the times, places and manner of holding elections for senators and representatives, shall be prescribed in each state by the legislature thereof. . . ." Oregon and the other states pointed out that in two major instances Congress had seen fit to establish uniform voter qualifications throughout the states—and it had done so by initiating constitutional amendments, rather than merely enacting a statute. In one of the amendments, the Nineteenth, the vote was extended to American women (see quote at left). And more recently, the Twenty-fourth Amendment outlawed the poll tax as a qualification for voting in national elections (see quote at left).

The right of citizens of the United States to vote shall not be denied or abridged by the United States or by any state on account of sex.

— 19th Amendment, U.S. Constitution (1920)

The right of citizens of the United States to vote in any primary or other election for President or Vice-President, for electors for President or Vice-President, or for senator or representative in Congress, shall not be denied or abridged by the United States or any state by reason of failure to pay any poll tax or other tax.

— 24th Amendment, U.S. Constitution (1964)

In its reply before the Supreme Court, the federal government also cited the same Article I, Section 4, of the Constitution used by the four states. Government lawyers reminded the Court that the passage, in full, read: "The times, places, and manner of holding elections for senators and representatives, shall be prescribed in each state by the legislature thereof; but the Congress may at any time, by law, make or alter such regulations, except as to the places of choosing senators."

The federal government based its case also on the equal protection clause of the Fourteenth Amendment. The argument was that Congress had sufficient evidence that American citizens between the ages of 18 and 21 were mature and responsible enough to vote. To deny them the right to vote was to deny them "equal protection of the laws." And clearly, contended the government, Congress had the power to enforce this clause by enacting "appropriate legislation."

FOR CRITICAL THINKING

1. Do you agree or disagree with the argument, made by Oregon and the three other states, that changes in voter-age qualifications should be made, if at all, by constitutional amendment—rather than by act of Congress? Explain your answer.
2. Do you agree or disagree with the argument, made by the federal government, that Article I, Section 4, of the Constitution gives Congress the power to establish voter-age qualifications? In all elections? Only in national elections? Explain your answers.
3. Do you agree or disagree with the argument that the equal protection clause gives Congress the power to extend the vote to 18-year-olds?
4. Do you believe young Americans between the ages of 18 and 21 are responsible enough to vote? Explain your answer.
5. How do you think the Supreme Court ruled in this case?

THORNBURG V. GINGLES (1986)

Legislative affairs in North Carolina had come a long way since the state's early years. In those days every time a new county was created in the western part of the state, one was divided in the east to make sure that coastal legislators kept the upper hand in numbers and in power. The state had also come a long way since the 1960's, when a court order forced rural legislators to draw districts based on population instead of geography. But in the 1980's a new issue arose. What happened when legislative districts were divided on the basis of population, but placed minority candidates at a disadvantage? The Supreme Court faced that subject in the following case.

Thornburg v. Gingles had its beginnings in 1981. That was when North Carolina's General Assembly reapportioned its legislative districts following the results of the 1980 census. Adhering to tradition, the plan called for both single-member and multi-member districts.

Angry civil rights leaders, including Ralph Gingles, claimed that the redistricting plan weakened the strength of black voters. In the case of one single-member seat, lawmakers split a concentration of black voters down the middle, creating two mostly white districts. Blacks comprised 22 percent of North Carolina's population, but only a handful of black legislators had ever been able to win election to the General Assembly. Racial gerrymandering had long been used to hold blacks back, critics charged. The new plan would continue the practice, with majority black areas that might have been able to elect their own candidates in single-member districts now being swallowed up by larger multi-member districts.

Black voters challenged the plan in court, saying it was contrary to a 1982 congressional amendment to the Voting Rights Act. That amendment outlawed any redistricting that had the effect of discriminating against black voters. It outlawed any voting procedure resulting "in a denial or abridgement of the right of any citizen of the United States to vote on account of race or color." A federal court agreed with their objections, saying that the use of multi-member districts in most cases illegally weakened minority voting strength. The court also cited the state's history of racial discrimination. Following this ruling, in 1984 the General Assembly redrew the lines of the contested districts, creating some single-member districts. Under this plan, voters elected 16 blacks to the 170-seat assembly.

Meanwhile, the issue sparked national interest when the Reagan administration joined Lacy Thornburg, North Carolina's attorney general, only to find itself pitted against a bipartisan congressional group headed by the Republican Majority Leader in the U.S. Senate, Robert Dole. Administration figures argued that the lower court was improperly trying to guarantee minorities a certain number of seats based on their percentage of the voting population. They also held that redistricting plans should be accepted under the Voting Rights Act. And clearly, since minorities were occasionally being elected to office in North Carolina, that was not the case.

Dole, meanwhile, filed a brief in court opposing Thornburg. Dole was an author of the 1982 congressional amendment to the Voting Rights Act. He felt that North Carolina's redistricting plan had deprived black voters of their rights, and urged the Supreme Court to overturn it.

FOR CRITICAL THINKING

1. Explain in your own words how gerrymandering works. Do you think that gerrymandering played a part in this case? Why or why not?
2. Should minorities be assured of representation roughly equal to their percentage of the voting population? Explain why or why not.
3. For what reasons might Senator Dole and other Republicans have challenged the Reagan administration's stand on this issue?
4. How do you think the Supreme Court ruled in this case?

EXPLORING THE MAIN IDEAS

WHAT DO YOU THINK?

1. How does the *Dred Scott* case illustrate the attitude of most whites toward blacks in the years before the Civil War? How was the decision of the Supreme Court in this case later set aside?
2. What does citizenship mean under our system of government? How do people acquire citizenship? How can they lose it?
3. In *Wesberry v. Sanders* (1964), the Supreme Court extended the *Baker* case principle to require "one man-one vote" equality in a state's congressional election districts. "As nearly as is practicable," said the Court, "one man's vote in a congressional election is to be worth as much as another's." Do you think this ruling was just and wise? Why or why not?
4. Which of the cases in this chapter do you consider the most just? Which do you consider the most unjust? Which do you think will have the greatest impact on problems confronting the United States today?

THINGS TO DO

1. Using sources that your instructor and your librarian may suggest, write a research paper on the important voter regulations in the following acts of Congress: (a) the Civil Rights Act of 1957, (b) the Civil Rights Act of 1960, and (c) the Voting Rights Act of 1965. From what you have learned so far in this book, indicate whether you believe each of these statutes is constitutional and why.
2. Using encyclopedias—plus other sources available to you—look up the main steps in the process of becoming a naturalized citizen. Incorporating as many of these steps as you see fit, write a one-act play about an alien immigrant becoming naturalized. Your instructor may wish to select the best play or plays for presentation in class.
3. Using procedures outlined in the back of this book, put on a mock trial of the *Korematsu* case.

Illustration Review

Now that you have finished this chapter's cases, re-analyze the pictures on pages 70–71. Which cases relate to which pictures? In what ways, if any, would your answers to the questions in "Illustration Analysis" at the beginning of the chapter now change? In what ways, if any, would your answers remain the same?

5 Equal Opportunity

Despite the Louisiana segregation law, Homer Plessy had made up his mind. On June 2, 1892, he bought a first-class ticket on the East Louisiana Railway for a train going from New Orleans to Covington—on the opposite side of Lake Pontchartrain. He walked through the railroad station and out past the car marked "for coloreds only." When he came to the coach marked "for whites only," he boarded it and eased into a vacant seat. This small act would lead to an historic Supreme Court case, one that would fix racial patterns for half a century.

Striding up to Plessy, the conductor asked him to leave the coach and go to the one assigned to "coloreds only." Plessy refused to budge. The conductor left and returned with a police officer. Forcibly ejected from the coach, Plessy was taken to the New Orleans jail and charged with violating an 1890 statute passed by the Louisiana General Assembly. The law read: "All railway companies carrying passengers in their coaches in this state shall provide equal but separate accommodations for the white and colored races. . . . No person or persons shall be permitted to occupy seats in coaches other than the ones assigned to them, on account of the race they belong to."

Plessy, who was black, had taken a seat on the "whites only" coach because he felt entitled to every right and privilege given white citizens. In court he contended that the Louisiana law had denied him "equal protection of the laws" under the Fourteenth Amendment. The Louisiana tribunal, however, upheld the constitutionality of the statute. Afterwards, Plessy appealed to the United States Supreme Court.

Justice Henry Brown wrote the Supreme Court's majority opinion in this case, *Plessy v. Ferguson* (1896). He argued that the object of the Fourteenth Amendment was to enforce the equality of the two races—but only before the law. It was not intended to enforce social equality.

The Louisiana legislature, said the Supreme Court, was free to make reasonable regulations of this sort under the state's police powers. And in deciding what was reasonable, the legislature could take into account "the established usages, customs, and traditions of the people," as well as "the preservation of the public peace and good order."

Justice Brown disagreed with Plessy's argument that segregation, or enforced separation of the races, "stamps the colored race with a badge of inferiority." If this were true, reasoned Brown, "it is not by reason of anything found in the act, but solely because the colored race chooses to put that construction upon it." This argument, he said, also assumes that "social prejudices may be overcome by legislation and that equal rights cannot be secured to the Negro except by an enforced [mixing] of the two races." Brown rejected the assumption. And, he added, "if the two races are to meet on terms of social equality, it must be the result of . . . appreciation of each other's merits and a voluntary consent of individuals. . . ." For these reasons, the Court upheld Louisiana's "equal but separate" law and ruled against Plessy.

Illustration Analysis

Analyze the pictures on pages 88–89. How do you think the illustration of the old train relates to this chapter? What mood is suggested by the torn edge in the photograph of the two women? What mood, by the jagged window? Which lines, shapes, and patterns in the entire design suggest separation, frustration, alienation?

IN YOUR OPINION

1. Do you agree or disagree with Justice Brown's majority opinion that segregation laws do not stamp blacks "with a badge of inferiority"? Explain.
2. What do you think "equal protection of the laws" means?
3. To what extent, if any, do you think the Fourteenth Amendment ought to protect the rights of citizens in education? In housing? In public accommodations, such as restaurants and hotels? Explain your answers.

14TH AMENDMENT: THE RISE AND FALL OF HOPE

All persons born or naturalized in the United States, and subject to the jurisdiction thereof are citizens of the United States and of the state wherein they reside. No state shall make or enforce any law which shall abridge the privileges or immunities of citizens of the United States; nor shall any state deprive any person of life, liberty, or property without due process of law; nor deny to any person within its jurisdiction the equal protection of the laws.

— 14th Amendment, U.S. Constitution (1868)

Plessy v. Ferguson came at the end of a half-century of dashed hopes for black Americans. After the Civil War (1861–1865), the young nation underwent a boom of growth that changed it into a powerful and complex giant. Free land, the Industrial Revolution, the rise of big business brought waves of immigrants flooding to its shores. Cities mushroomed. Amid all this growth, America failed to heal the bitter wounds left by the war between North and South. And the forgotten ex-slaves, freed in war, witnessed in peacetime the forces of segregation washing away many of their new liberties.

For four million ex-slaves, the postwar era began on a note of high hope. The Fourteenth Amendment in 1868 held out a promise of full citizenship (see quote at left). It defined "citizens of the United States" in a way to include blacks—thus nullifying the *Dred Scott* decision on the point.

PRIVILEGES AND IMMUNITIES

The Fourteenth Amendment also prohibited any state from interfering with the "privileges or immunities" of United States citizens. What did this mean? To the amendment's sponsor, Representative John A. Bingham of Ohio, the privileges and immunities clause referred to the liberties guaranteed under the Bill of Rights.

In *Barron v. Baltimore* (1833), the Supreme Court had ruled that the first ten amendments to the Constitution were protected only against interference by the federal government. Bingham, strongly opposed to such a narrow ruling, insisted that the Fourteenth Amendment protected Bill of Rights liberties against state interference as well. Five years after adoption, however, the first Supreme Court case interpreting the amendment rejected this idea in the *Slaughter-House Cases* (1873). The Fourteenth Amendment, the Court held, was designed chiefly to protect citizenship rights of ex-slaves.

"Equal protection of the laws" places all upon a footing of legal equality and gives the same protection to all for the preservation of life, liberty and property, and the pursuit of happiness.

— Justice Swayne, *Slaughter-House Cases* (1873)

Down through the years, in a number of separate cases, the Supreme Court eventually expanded coverage of the Fourteenth to include all persons—and protect most of the Bill of Rights' "fundamental liberties" against invasion by the states (see introductory chapter). But for a good many years after the *Slaughter-House Cases* were decided, the Fourteenth Amendment was narrowly interpreted.

DUE PROCESS OF LAW

Two other passages have loomed as the vital power-clauses of the Fourteenth. The due process clause, applying selective Bill of Rights liberties to the states, barred a state from taking any person's "life, liberty, or property without due process of law." Due process means all the proper steps required for a fair hearing in a legal proceeding. The other clause, the equal protection clause, prohibited a state from denying any citizen "equal protection of the laws." For blacks, here was the heart of the Fourteenth Amendment, the potential keystone upon which would rest their historic quest for equal rights.

BACKGROUND OF EQUAL PROTECTION

The Fourteenth Amendment provides the first clear reference to equal rights anywhere in the Constitution. True, the Declaration of Independence in 1776 had proclaimed as a fundamental American principle "that all men are created equal." Of course, this did not imply that all persons were equal in skills or strength. It simply meant that all persons should be treated equally by the government. The concept of equality before the law, however, was not spelled out in the original Constitution. That had to wait for the equal protection clause.

REASONABLE CLASSIFICATION

Equal protection is the most important single principle that any nation can take as its ideal.

— Justice Douglas, *We the Judges* (1955)

Even these words, "equal protection of the laws," do not require a state law to apply to each and every person. A law could constitutionally apply to a special class of persons or groups. It could, for instance, apply to railroads. Or it could apply to burglars. But the category, or class, had to be "reasonable." A law would not be valid if, for example, it levied a tax on blue-eyed homeowners. The category could not be so unequal that it was completely discriminatory.

STATE ACTION

Individual invasion of individual rights is not the subject matter of the [14th] Amendment. It has a deeper and broader scope. It nullifies and makes void all state legislation, and state action of every kind, which impairs the privileges and immunities of citizens of the United States, or which injures them in life, liberty or property without due process of law, or which denies to any of them the equal protection of the laws.

— Justice Bradley, *The Civil Rights Cases* (1883)

Besides reasonable classification, the Supreme Court has placed another restriction on the equal protection clause. The rule arose in the *Civil Rights Cases* of 1883. Here the Court held unconstitutional sections of the Civil Rights Act of 1875. That law made it a crime for one person to deprive another of the "full and equal enjoyment of the accommodations, advantages, facilities, and privileges of inns, public conveyances on land or water, theatres, and other places of public amusement." The 1875 provisions were based on the Fourteenth. The Supreme Court, however, ruled that the amendment was limited to "state action." It did not apply to action by individuals.

ARRIVAL OF SEGREGATION

The *Civil Rights Cases* reflected the mood of the times. The federal government was tiring of the "Negro question." White Southerners were donning the hood and robe of the Ku Klux Klan; by night they were riding to whip and hang and terrorize blacks from asserting their civil rights. Eventually white voters recaptured political control of state governments across the South. And in 1877 the United States withdrew the last of its Reconstruction troops. Encouraged by the Supreme Court's position in the *Civil Rights Cases,* southern states began passing laws rigidly segregating the races. The former slaves increasingly found themselves legally restricted to separate schools, housing, and public facilities. Then, in 1896, came the *Plessy* case. It put America's highest judicial stamp of approval on second-class citizenship for black people. The case, indeed, was the culmination of decades of dashed hopes. And its doctrine, "separate but equal," would prevail for another half-century.

BROWN V. BOARD OF EDUCATION (1954)

Education is a pivotal value in the United States. Traditionally, the public school system has passed down the ideal of democracy to each new generation. It has also served as a unifying band for the nation's many ethnic groups.

Yet opportunity in education historically has not been equal. As early after the Civil War as the 1870's, southern and border states began setting up separate schools for blacks. Based on the Plessy *doctrine of "separate but equal," state laws made segregated education the prevailing pattern by the turn of the century. Schools for blacks, however, were hardly "equal."*

By the 1930's, most southern states were spending only about a third as much for the education of a black pupil as for a white pupil. During that decade, the U.S. Supreme Court began to insist upon "substantial equality" in education. In Missouri ex rel. Gaines v. Canada *(1938), the Court ruled that state creation of a law school for whites but none for blacks violated the Fourteenth Amendment. In the following case, which some constitutional experts have called the most important of the twentieth century, the Supreme Court agreed to decide whether segregated public schools were inherently unequal. The 58-year-old "separate but equal" doctrine, established by* Plessy v. Ferguson, *was about to be tested.*

In Topeka, Kansas, Oliver Brown watched his children start out for school, and bitter resentment welled up within him. Every day they faced a long bus ride across town to a distant elementary school—despite the fact that another elementary school, an all white one, was much closer to their house. The children suffered this inconvenience for one reason: they were black.

The Kansas legislature had passed a statute allowing cities with a population of 15,000 or more to maintain separate elementary and junior high schools for black and white students. The Board of Education in Topeka consequently had established 18 schools for whites, 4 for blacks.

Angered, Mr. and Mrs. Brown brought suit in a federal district court. They sought an injunction to prevent enforcement of the state statute. They claimed that the schools their children attended were inferior to the white public schools. And since such segregated schools were not "equal" and could not be made "equal," they were deprived of "equal protection of the laws" under the Fourteenth Amendment.

The federal district court in Kansas considered as precedents two cases decided by the Supreme Court in 1950. One was *Sweatt v. Painter,* which ruled that segregated law schools run by the state of Texas were unconstitutional. The other was *McLaurin v. Oklahoma State Regents.* Here the court made a similar ruling in the case of a black graduate school student. He had been forced (1) to attend class in a separate room from his white classmates and (2) to eat in the university cafeteria at a different time from white students. The Supreme Court held that these segregation practices were unconstitutional. The federal district court in Kansas said that it was "difficult to see why" these rulings, based on the Fourteenth Amendment, should not also apply to the lower grades.

Nevertheless, the Browns were denied their injunction. In comparing Topeka's white and black schools, the district court found "substantial equality" in buildings, programs of study, qualifications and salaries of teachers. Moreover, said the district court, in spite of the *Sweatt* and the *McLaurin* cases, *Plessy v. Ferguson* "has not been [completely] overruled and . . . it still presents authority for maintenance of segregated schools in lower grades."

The Browns sought review by the U.S. Supreme Court.

FOR CRITICAL THINKING

1. What factors did the federal district court in this case find substantially equal in the white and black schools of Topeka? What other types of factors, if any, might not be equal?
2. To what extent, if any, do you think the *Sweatt* case should apply here? To what extent, if any, should the *McLaurin* case apply? Explain your answers.
3. To what extent, if any, should the "separate but equal" doctrine of the *Plessy* case apply?
4. Does the quotation from Chief Justice Warren at left help you decide this case? Explain. Do you think it is from a majority or a dissenting opinion? Why?
5. How do you think the Supreme Court ruled in this case?

To separate [black students] from others of similar age and qualifications solely because of their race generates a feeling of inferiority as to their status in the community that may affect their hearts and minds in a way unlikely ever to be undone.

— Chief Justice Warren, *Brown v. Board of Education* (1954)

FRONTIERO V. RICHARDSON (1973)

The long struggle toward equal opportunity for women did not end with the Nineteenth Amendment—which in 1920 granted them the right to vote. In a sense, that was only a beginning. Throughout the United States in the nineteenth century, women had been typically denied such basic legal rights as holding public office, serving on juries, starting a lawsuit in their own name, sometimes even owning, buying, and selling property in their own name. Dedicated crusaders began to overturn such discrimination on many fronts. Many cases overturning

No state shall . . . deny to any person within its jurisdiction the equal protection of the laws.

— 14th Amendment, U.S. Constitution (1868)

sex discrimination were decided under the equal protection clause of the Fourteenth Amendment (see quote, left) or other amendments. In 1971, for instance, the U.S. Supreme Court in Phillips v. Martin Marietta Corporation *(1971) ruled in favor of Ida Phillips, who complained that she had been refused a job by Martin Marietta because she had preschool children—even though the company hired men with preschool children. The Court interpreted the Civil Rights Act of 1964 clause making it an "unfair employment practice for an employer to . . . refuse to hire" a person because of sex. Then, in 1973 came this case.*

Sharron Frontiero, a lieutenant in the U.S. Air Force, was angry. She protested that certain military regulations discriminated against her as a woman.

Lt. Frontiero had applied for increased pay—as housing and medical allowances—on the grounds that her husband Joseph was her "dependent." Such fringe benefits were automatically granted to a male member of the armed services for his wife. But Lt. Frontiero was turned down because she had not proven that her husband was indeed dependent on her for more than one-half his support.

At that time, Joseph Frontiero was a full-time student at Huntingdon College in Montgomery, Alabama. His living expenses, including his share of the household expenses, totalled approximately $354 per month. He received $205 per month in veterans' benefits. This income from the federal government, because of his previous military service, Frontiero contributed toward the running of the household.

Lt. Frontiero brought suit against Secretary of Defense Elliott Richardson. She cited two federal laws that discriminated against her:

1. "The Career Compensation Act of 1949," which established a uniform pattern of military pay and allowances. The law said that a female member of the armed services had to prove her husband's dependency.
2. "The Dependent Medical Care Act of 1956," which was designed to make uniform regulations for medical services to military personnel. This law required female members of the armed services again to prove their husband's dependency.

Lt. Frontiero argued that these statutes conflicted with the Fifth Amendment (see quote, page 96), which forbids discrimination that is "so unjustifiable as to be violative of due process." In her argument against the laws, she declared:

a. That laws were unfair as a matter of procedure. They required a female member of the armed services to prove her husband's dependency. A male member did not have to do this.

b. The laws were unfair in substance. A male member of the armed services who does not provide more than half his wife's support receives benefits. A female member is denied such benefits.

The defendant argued that the preference in the two laws for male applicants was "reasonable." Men, as a general rule, said the defendants, know more about business affairs than women. Since women have not, as yet, engaged in politics, the professions, business or industry to the extent that men have, men are generally more capable as administrators than women.

No person shall be held to answer for a capital, or otherwise infamous crime, unless on presentment or indictment of a grand jury, except in cases arising in the land or naval forces, or in the militia, when in actual service in time of war or public danger; nor shall any person be subject for the same offense to be twice put in jeopardy of life or limb; nor shall be compelled in any criminal case to be a witness against himself, nor be deprived of life, liberty, or property, without due process of law; nor shall private property be taken for public use without just compensation.

— 5th Amendment, U.S. Constitution (1791)

A federal court ruled against Lt. Frontiero. The court reasoned that the husband generally is the breadwinner in the family and the wife the dependent partner. It is more economical to require only female members of the armed forces claiming husbands to prove their actual dependency than to have both men and women offer proof of dependency. (Roughly 99 percent of uniformed service personnel at that time were male.) Such differing treatment probably saved a lot of administrative expense. The case was eventually heard by the U.S. Supreme Court.

FOR CRITICAL THINKING

1. What is the main issue in this case?
2. What do you think are the best arguments for Lt. Frontiero? Against her?
3. In what way, if any, do you think the Fifth Amendment (left) should apply to this case?
4. How do you think the Supreme Court ruled in this case?

WYGANT V. JACKSON BOARD OF EDUCATION (1986)

One goal of civil rights leaders in the 1960's was to make sure that the courts upheld the Fourteenth Amendment's guarantee of "equal protection." But laws alone could not give all Americans an equal chance to compete in life. Increasingly, efforts were made to see that "equal opportunity" became a reality.

Accordingly, the federal government began to adopt affirmative action policies. These policies required businesses and schools that received federal funds to recruit minorities and women. Affirmative action programs were designed to implement federal anti-discrimination laws.

Critics of some affirmative action programs have charged that preference given to minorities and women amounted to reverse discrimination. With affirmative action becoming a heated topic, a number of controversial cases came before the Supreme Court. In some instances, the Court allowed the use of affirmative action to make up for past discrimination. In Local 28, Sheet Metal Workers v. EEOC *(1986), it agreed with a lower court order directing a New York union that had refused to admit blacks to have a 29 percent non-white membership within a year's time. In 1986 the Court also upheld a Cleveland plan to promote one minority firefighter for every white who received a promotion (*Local 93 v. City of Cleveland*).*

In other cases the Court put limits on affirmative action plans. In Firefighters Local Union No. 1784 v. Stotts *(1984) the Court heard the case of three Memphis whites who had been laid off even though they had more seniority than blacks whose jobs were saved. Because this violated the "last hired, first fired" clause of the union contract—and because that contract did not discriminate against blacks—the Court agreed with the white firefighters. A similar case involved a teacher layoff plan.*

It was 1985 and Wendy Wygant was furious. The Jackson, Michigan, kindergarten teacher had been laid off seven times in the last eight years, including two full school years.

"I've lost years of my income," she told an interviewer, as she headed into court. Along with seven other teachers who had been laid off more than once, she was bringing a suit to halt the layoffs. The reason that they had been laid off, the teachers charged, was solely because they were white.

In the past, almost all the teachers in Jackson were white. There were a handful of black teachers, but because they had little seniority, they almost always lost their jobs when there were layoffs for budgetary reasons. Then, due to these layoffs, in 1972 Jackson was beset by racial tension. In response, the Board of Education suggested to the teacher's union that a layoff plan be added to its contract. The board and the union eventually approved a provision that would protect minority teachers against layoffs. They also sought to ensure that the Jackson schools had effective "role models" for minority children.

Wygant and the other white teachers argued that the affirmative action provision was not fair. The plan allowed the board to take away jobs from innocent people who had not practiced discrimination. And none of the black teachers allowed to keep their jobs was necessarily a victim of discrimination. Why not use less severe methods to achieve integration, such as the adoption of voluntary hiring goals?

The school board responded that there had in fact been past discrimination. Now the school district had an obligation to correct the damage that had been done. Maintaining an integrated teaching staff was one way in which the schools could do so. Certainly, the board went on, the white teachers' loss of work was regrettable. But it is not unusual for innocent people to be disadvantaged by laws that promote the general welfare. Taking away a person's home to make way for a stadium or a highway is an example of such a law.

A district court dismissed the white teachers' claims, as did the Court of Appeals. The case then went to the Supreme Court.

FOR CRITICAL THINKING

1. What are the goals of affirmative action? Why were affirmative action plans started?
2. Why did the Jackson Board of Education institute an affirmative

action program? What part did the teacher's union play in the affirmative action program?

3. In your opinion, which side had the stronger argument in this case—the board of education or the white teachers? Explain.
4. How do you think the Supreme Court ruled in this case?

ROTARY INTERNATIONAL V. ROTARY CLUB OF DUARTE (1987)

In 1972 Congress passed the Equal Rights Amendment, declaring that "equality of rights under the law shall not be denied or abridged by the United States in any state on account of sex." Ten years later, when its extended time limit ran out, the amendment was three states short of ratification.

*Since then, in the absence of a specific constitutional provision such as ERA, the Supreme Court has stopped short of declaring that all laws treating women as a separate class must be questioned. In some cases the Supreme Court has upheld laws discriminating between men and women. For instance, it upheld a Florida law that granted widows, but not widowers, a yearly $500 tax exemption (*Kahn v. Shevin, *1974). On the other hand, it found unconstitutional a New York law that permitted unwed mothers, but not unwed fathers, to prevent the adoption of their children (*Caban v. Mohammed, *1979). And the Court ruled against a women-only admissions policy at a state-supported nursing school (*Mississippi University for Women v. Hogan, *1982). Then, in 1987, the Court heard a case involving the practices of a private club.*

The Rotary Club of Duarte, California, was in a quandary. The club, which had been losing members, had adopted a new membership policy. It had admitted three local businesswomen—Donna Nogart, Mary Lou Elliott, and Rosemary Freitag—as active members. By so doing, however, it had broken the rules of Rotary International, its parent organization. A worldwide body of more than 19,000 clubs with 900,000 members in 157 countries, Rotary International had always had an all-male policy. Now it responded by revoking the Duarte club's charter. The local club answered with a lawsuit.

In court, the Duarte club's lawyer, Judith Resnick, stated that California had strict laws barring sex discrimination by private clubs. Those laws should be upheld. The Constitution, she argued, does not protect sex discrimination by all-male private clubs, particularly those—like Rotary—that are often used for business. By not allowing businesswomen in Rotary, she said, "The message to us is we're second-class citizens." A California appellate court agreed with the Duarte club, ordering Rotary International to reinstate its charter.

Rotary International fought back, taking the case to the Supreme Court. It said that the First Amendment's right of free association entitles a private club like Rotary to choose its membership—even if that means excluding women. It claimed that its selective membership policy, as well as the many public service activities it performed in the community, entitled it to First Amendment protection of its right to set its own membership requirements. Finally, it pointed out that there is no federal law against sex discrimination by private clubs. It acknowledged, however, that about half the states—including California—have laws banning sex discrimination in business establishments and public accommodations.

FOR CRITICAL THINKING

1. What reasons do you think Rotary International had for not admitting women?
2. Do you think all private organizations should be allowed to determine their own membership? Should size be a consideration? Explain.
3. Why would exclusion from Rotary make women feel like "second-class citizens"? How might it affect their chances in business?
4. How do you think the Supreme Court ruled in this case?

EXPLORING THE MAIN IDEAS

WHAT DO YOU THINK?

1. Which do you think is the most important case in this chapter? Why?
2. How are the *Plessy* and *Brown* cases alike? How are they different? How do you account for the differences?
3. Do you think all laws treating women as a separate class should be questioned? Why or why not?

Illustration Review

Now that you have finished this chapter's cases, re-analyze the pictures on pages 88–89. Which cases relate to which pictures? In what ways, if any, would your answers to the questions in "Illustration Analysis" at the beginning of the chapter now change? In what ways, if any, would your answers remain the same?

THINGS TO DO

1. Write a short history of the struggle for American women's rights.
2. Using procedures outlined in the back of this book, put on a mock trial of *Brown v. Board of Education.*

6 Rights of the Accused

Beyond Chattanooga, the Alabama Great Southern freight train puffed lazily through the Appalachian foothills of Tennessee. It meandered southwest, in the direction of Scottsboro, Alabama. Aboard the boxcars lolled motley groups of hoboes. This was the spring of 1931, a rough year in the Great Depression; and they were all—black boys and white boys alike—bumming across the South in search of work. Among the hoboes were two young white women. Dressed in men's overalls, they had been sleeping in tramp havens and railroad yards and hopping freights from place to place.

Shortly after the train emerged from a tunnel through Lookout Mountain, an argument began between some black and white youths. The young women were not involved. Eventually, a scuffle erupted, and the blacks threw the whites off the slow-moving freight. The angry whites, seeking revenge, reported the incident to Alabama authorities.

When the freight clacked in to Point Rock, Alabama, a white posse was waiting. Shotguns and pistols drawn, they hauled nine black youths off the train and tied them with ropes. A half-dozen whites were also rounded up from the boxcars—including the two young women in overalls.

The black youths, ages 13 to 20, were taken to the nearby county seat, Scottsboro. Outside the jail, a noisy mob gathered. Inside, the frightened prisoners were being questioned by sheriffs' deputies. Suddenly, a man brought in the two young white women in overalls.

"Do you know these girls?" he demanded.

"No," responded one of the blacks. As far as he knew, none of his eight fellow prisoners had ever seen them before they were hauled off the train at Point Rock.

"No," said the other blacks.

"*No*?" thundered the white man. "You *raped* these girls!"

Thus began the "Scottsboro Cases." One of the white women, questioned by authorities, claimed that she and her companion had been repeatedly raped by the nine prisoners. Hasty trials of the youths were completed in three days. They had no adequate defense counsel. The nine were convicted by an all-white jury. Eight of them were sentenced to death and one to life imprisonment.

This incident attracted international publicity. Communist organizations—seizing this chance to dramatize the oppression of blacks in America—managed to get themselves involved in the defense of the "Scottsboro Boys."

Twice, the affair spawned landmark constitutional cases that went all the way to the U.S. Supreme Court. In the first of these, *Powell v. Alabama* (1932), the Court reversed the convictions on the grounds that the defendants had not had adequate legal counsel. The due process clause of the Fourteenth Amendment, ruled the Court, demands that a defendant in a state criminal case punishable by death be represented by an attorney—regardless of whether one is requested.

New trials took place in 1933. One of the young women then testified that the story of rape had been a lie. Nevertheless, all the black defendants again were convicted in Alabama—and this time all were sentenced to die.

During the second round of trials, one of the "Scottsboro Boys," Clarence Norris, claimed that his rights under the Fourteenth Amendment had been violated because blacks had been systematically excluded from the jury that convicted him. Norris produced evidence showing that "in a long number of years no Negro had been called for jury service in that county." Although the preliminary jury list contained names of blacks, officials designated them as "colored" on that list. And names of such blacks never appeared on the final jury roll. Apparently, their names had been eliminated without their qualifications for jury duty ever having been considered. Testimony further indicated that there were blacks in the county qualified for jury service.

The state of Alabama replied that even if blacks were not listed on the final jury roll, it could not be proved that race or color had caused the omission. In this case, said the state, no one had been excluded because of race or color.

After Norris' conviction, he raised the "systematic exclusion" issue before the Alabama Supreme Court. His conviction was affirmed. Next, in the case of *Norris v. Alabama* (1935), he appealed to the U.S. Supreme Court, which ruled in his favor. The Court held that systematic exclusion of all blacks from a grand jury or from a trial jury in a state criminal case was denial of "equal protection of the laws" guaranteed under the Fourteenth Amendment.

Illustration Analysis

Analyze the pictures on pages 100–101. What idea, if any, is communicated by the special treatment used on the photograph of the arrest scene at center? What is symbolized by the special treatment of the prisoner in the upper right corner? How do you think the electronic "bug" inside the fake olive of the cocktail glass relates to this chapter? To what constitutional right is such a device related? What other elements in this design are related to the same right? To what constitutional rights are the other illustrations in this design related?

IN YOUR OPINION

1. In what ways can a lawyer assist a defendant in a criminal case? Is this help essential to a fair trial? Do you think the state should be required to furnish lawyers for defendants in criminal cases other than those punishable by death? Explain your answers.
2. Do you believe that freedom from racial discrimination in the selection of a jury is essential to a fair trial? Why?
3. What rights under our system of government do you consider essential to guarantee the accused a fair trial? Why?

CRIME AND CONSTITUTIONAL LIBERTIES

In the 1930's, states varied widely in their criminal trial procedures—and in the rights granted the accused. The U.S. Supreme Court began dramatically expanding its role as the Constitution's watchdog over such matters. Increasingly, it applied the Bill of Rights to state trials—just as it always had to federal criminal prosecutions. Standards for "fair trial" became uniform and predictable across the nation. In our legal system, one vital element of "fair trial" is an impartial jury—which was at stake in *Norris v. Alabama.* Another, naturally, is an impartial judge.

RIGHT TO COUNSEL

Still another critical ingredient in our Anglo-American heritage of "fair trial" has been the right of the accused to a lawyer. This ancient right, guaranteed by the Sixth Amendment (see quote at

In all criminal prosecutions, the accused shall enjoy the right . . . to have the assistance of counsel for his defense.

— 6th Amendment, U.S. Constitution (1791)

left) was involved in *Powell v. Alabama.* Since that time, protection of this right has been vastly enlarged by the Supreme Court—as several cases in this chapter will show.

SELF-INCRIMINATION

No person shall be . . . compelled in any criminal case to be a witness against himself. . . .

— 5th Amendment, U.S. Constitution (1791)

The privilege against **self-incrimination**—in other words, the right to remain silent—is protected by the Fifth Amendment (see quote at left). Still another key element of "fair trial," this ancient privilege guarantees that accused persons, unless they so desire, need not take the witness stand in their own defense and thereby subject themselves to cross-examination by the prosecuting attorney. The privilege also is intended to prevent the police from forcing the accused to make a confession.

PROCESS OF CRIMINAL JUSTICE

At what stages in the "process of criminal justice", should the important rights of the Fifth and Sixth Amendments operate? This process varies somewhat from state to state. But, generally speaking, there are at least eight distinct stages: (1) **investigation**—which, if it leads to an arrest, may continue until the trial; (2) **arrest**—that is, the authorities taking a suspect into physical custody; (3) **booking**—that is, fingerprinting and photographing the suspect and recording his or her arrest at the police station; (4) **appearance**—before a magistrate, or judge, who determines whether to keep suspects in jail until trial, or whether to let them go free on "bail" (security, usually money, forfeited if the suspect fails to appear for trial); (5) **formal charge** of a crime—either an "indictment" presented by a grand jury or, more frequently, an "information" filed by the prosecuting attorney; (6) **arraignment** in court, where the accused enters a plea of "guilty" or "not guilty" to the formal charge; (7) **trial;** and (8) **appeal.**

RIGHT TO PRIVACY

The right of the people to be secure in their persons, houses, papers, and effects, against unreasonable searches and seizures, shall not be violated; and no warrants shall issue but upon probable cause, supported by oath or affirmation, and particularly describing the place to be searched, and the persons or things to be seized.

— 4th Amendment, U.S. Constitution (1791)

In the early stages, especially during investigation and arrest, the great and precious guarantees of the Fourth Amendment (see quote at left) come into play. First, the amendment, in effect, recognizes the ancient Anglo-American legal principle that citizens have a right to privacy—to be protected against undue interference by their government. In general terms, the Fourth Amendment prohibits "unreasonable searches and seizures." Then, it spells out the conditions that must be observed to ensure the legality of search warrants—"no warrants shall issue but upon probable cause . . . particularly describing the place to be searched, and the persons or things to be seized." The Supreme Court traditionally has been tenacious in upholding these limitations. If a law officer has violated them, any evidence illegally obtained may not be used in court—state or federal.

The makers of our Constitution undertook . . . to protect Americans in their beliefs, their thoughts, their emotions and their sensations. They conferred, as against the government, the right to be let alone—the most comprehensive of rights and the right most valued by civilized man. To protect that right, every unjustifiable intrusion by the government upon the privacy of the individual, whatever the means employed, must be deemed a violation of the Fourth Amendment.

— Justice Brandeis, *Olmstead v. United States* (1928)

Historically, America has had to deal with strong tensions in ensuring the right to privacy. In case after case, the right of the individual to be left alone had to be balanced with the right of society to gather evidence against crime. And during periods of mounting criminal activity, the tension usually escalates. For at such times, the government is likely to seek to enlarge its powers of "search and seizure."

SMUGGLING IN THE COLONIES

Two such periods stand out in America's past. Smuggling by colonial merchants became rampant during the years just before the Revolutionary War. The merchants used this approach to escape the taxes and restrictions imposed by Parliament on colonial trade. Royal customs officials fought back, using "writs of assistance"—warrants written so broadly that they allowed almost unlimited searches for the smuggled goods.

In the *Writs of Assistance Case* (1761), James Otis, representing a group of outraged Massachusetts Bay merchants, attacked the writs as being against "fundamental principles of law." Declared the young and eloquent lawyer, "A man who is quiet is as secure in his house as a prince in his castle." Nevertheless, the Massachusetts court upheld the hated writs, and their continued use was a major factor leading to revolution.

PROHIBITION AND CRIME

About a century and a half later during national prohibition (1919–1933), smuggling flourished once again. Making, selling, or drinking alcoholic beverages was against federal law. Violation of the law was widespread—there were more than a million arrests. In one famous case, *Dumbra v. United States* (1925), the Supreme Court upheld a federal warrant to search for and seize illegal liquor. And the opinion laid down a landmark definition of "probable cause": there had to be reasonable ground for suspicion, on the part of a normally prudent person, that the suspected crime had actually been committed.

Despite efforts at enforcement, smuggled whiskey continued to pour across the nation's borders. Home manufacture mushroomed—"bathtub gin" was in high fashion. Frustrated federal investigators, desperate for evidence, for the first time began tapping private telephone lines. And thus started what many critics believe is the greatest of all modern threats to the right of privacy—electronic eavesdropping.

GIDEON V. WAINWRIGHT (1963)

Before the 1930's, states generally were under no obligation to furnish lawyers to poor people accused of crimes. The Sixth Amendment was interpreted to mean that a person was entitled to have legal representation—if he or she could afford to hire a lawyer. The "Scottsboro Case" of Powell v. Alabama *(1932) changed all that. Here the Supreme Court ruled that a state in a capital case—a case in which the maximum penalty is death—had to furnish a poor person with free and competent legal counsel. That broke new ground. Then, six years later, in* Johnson v. Zerbst *(1938), free counsel was guaranteed to such defendants in all federal criminal prosecutions. The extension of this rule to states, however, was turned down in* Betts v. Brady *(1942). Now the Supreme Court drew the line—declaring that penniless defendants, in noncapital state prosecutions, had no right under the Constitution to a free attorney. Then came the following case, a modern classic.*

The Bay Harbor Poolroom in Panama City, Florida, closed down at midnight. The proprietor locked all the doors and windows—carefully, for the neighborhood was a hangout for vagrants, drunks, and petty gamblers. Sometime after dawn, a police officer on a routine patrol discovered that a window of the poolroom had been smashed. Inside, the jukebox and cigarette machine had been broken into, and some beer and wine were missing.

Shortly afterwards, on a tip from a bystander who had "stayed out all night," police arrested Clarence Earl Gideon. Gideon, who lived in a hotel across the street from the poolroom, was the portrait of a loser: age 51, four times a convict, three times married, drifter, gambler—prematurely white-haired, with a frail, tuberculosis-wracked body. Yet the loser refused, this time, to lose. From the outset, Clarence Gideon steadfastly protested his innocence of the charge of "breaking and entering." And thus, from these seedy origins, began one of the most celebrated cases in the annals of the Supreme Court.

At his trial, Gideon asked to have the Florida court provide him a lawyer free because he did not have enough money to hire his own. To this the judge replied: "Mr. Gideon, I am sorry, but I cannot appoint counsel to represent you in this case. Under the laws of the state of Florida, the only time the court can appoint counsel to represent a defendant is when that person is charged with a capital offense." The charge against Gideon, "breaking and entering with the intent to commit a misdemeanor," was not a capital crime—that is, one punishable by death. Gideon protested, "The United States Supreme Court says I am entitled to be represented by counsel." But his request was denied by the Florida court.

Without a lawyer to represent him and untrained in the law himself, Gideon conducted his own defense about as well as could be expected for a layman. But he was ineffective. He cross-examined the state's main witness, the tipster who said he had seen Gideon inside the poolroom at 5:30 on the morning it was broken into. But Gideon failed to question the tipster thoroughly about what he himself was doing outside the poolroom at the early hour. Nor did he question the man about his reputation, this would surely have been explored by a skilled attorney.

After cross-examining one other witness for the prosecution, the owner of the poolroom, Gideon presented eight witnesses of his own. But his questioning of these witnesses was so rambling that it produced nothing decisively helpful to his defense. In his final argument to the jury, Gideon simply stressed his innocence.

The jury found Clarence Earl Gideon guilty. And the judge sentenced him to five years in state prison. Gideon asked the Supreme Court of Florida for a writ of habeas corpus. But the writ was denied.

No state shall deprive any person of life, liberty, or property, without due process of law. . . .

— 14th Amendment, U.S. Constitution (1868)

While in prison, Gideon prepared and submitted a five-page "pauper's petition," asking the Supreme Court to review his case. Gideon said his conviction violated the due process clause of the Fourteenth Amendment (see quote at left). To try poor people for a felony (crime punishable by imprisonment of one year or more) without providing them with lawyers, said Gideon, was to deprive them of "due process of law."

FOR CRITICAL THINKING

1. How effective was Gideon in serving as his own lawyer at the trial? How effective would the average defendant be in a similar situation? What things, if any, is a lawyer able to do at a trial that a client cannot do in his or her own defense? Do you think a lawyer's help in a criminal case is a necessity or a luxury? Why?

There can be no equal justice where the kind of trial a man gets depends on the amount of money he has.

— Justice Black, *Griffin v. Illinois* (1956)

2. Does the government in a criminal prosecution always employ lawyers? What bearing, if any, should that have on this case?

3. Does the quotation from Justice Black (at left) help you decide this case? Explain.

4. Do you think a state should have to provide free legal counsel for defendants too poor to hire a lawyer? If no, why? If yes, for what offenses? All? Murder? Robbery? Traffic violations?

5. How do you think the Supreme Court ruled in this case?

MIRANDA V. ARIZONA (1966)

The privilege against self-incrimination has roots in seventeenth-century England. It began as a reaction to the excesses of the hated Star Chamber—where royal interrogators persuaded prisoners, by torture and by threat, to confess to crimes. Under our own Fifth Amendment, the privilege has long guaranteed that defendants in a criminal case need not take the stand in their own defense. It also protects any other witnesses from having to answer questions that would tend to implicate them in a criminal offense. Until recent years, this right to remain silent was traditionally limited to interrogations under oath—as in criminal and civil trials, grand juries, congressional committees. But what about police questioning during pretrial stages? Such interrogation was not conducted under oath. And it frequently led to confession, sometimes under dubious circumstances. The issue arose in the following landmark case.

March 3, 1963: the telephone at the Phoenix Police Department jangled—an urgent call like hundreds of others that day. This one, however, was the curtain-ringer for one of the most controversial cases in modern Supreme Court history. The call came from the angry family of an 18-year-old woman who claimed that she had just been raped.

According to the woman, she was on her way home from her job at a local movie theater when a car pulled up. A man got out, she said, grabbed her, threw her into the back seat, and tied her hands and feet. The man, whom she had never seen before, drove for about twenty minutes. When he stopped the car, she said, he untied her and raped her. He then drove back to the area where be had picked her up and let her out of the car.

Ten days later, Phoenix police picked up Ernesto Miranda, a 23-year-old drifter, at his home and took him to the police station. He was placed in a "line-up" with four other men—all about the same age and build. The woman identified him as the man who had attacked her.

Miranda was then taken to an interrogation room and questioned by two police officers. Two hours later, the officers emerged from the room with a written confession signed by Miranda.

At Miranda's trial, the two officers testified before a jury that during Miranda's interrogation he admitted that he forced the woman into his car, drove away with her, and raped her. The officers said they then asked him to prepare a written confession. At this time, the officers claimed that they read to Miranda a statement typed at the top of the confession form. The statement said that the confession was made voluntarily, without threats or promises of immunity and "with full knowledge of my legal rights, understanding any statements I make may be used against me." The officer who had read this statement aloud to Miranda admitted, however, that it did not say that the person confessing was entitled to an attorney.

No person shall be . . . compelled in any criminal case to be a witness against himself. . . .

— 5th Amendment, U.S. Constitution (1791)

Miranda was found guilty of kidnapping and rape. He was sentenced to twenty to thirty years in prison.

Miranda appealed his case to the Arizona Supreme Court. The issue arose whether his written confession should have been admitted into evidence. Miranda did not have an attorney at the time the statement was made and signed. Therefore, had he been deprived of his right to remain silent under the Fifth Amendment and his right to counsel under the Sixth Amendment (see quotes at left)?

In all criminal prosecutions, the accused shall enjoy the right . . . to have the assistance of counsel for his defense.

— 6th Amendment, U.S. Constitution (1791)

The state declared that Miranda had made his statement voluntarily; no threats or use of force or coercion, no promises of immunity had been made. Arizona claimed that the prisoner understood his legal rights and that the statement he made could be used against him. It was true that Miranda had no attorney at the time he made his statement. But, said the state, he did not specifically request counsel. The Arizona Supreme Court affirmed Miranda's conviction. It held that his constitutional rights had not been violated in obtaining the confession and that it was proper to admit the statement in evidence. The case then went to the U.S. Supreme Court.

[Our system of criminal justice] demands that the government seeking to punish an individual produce the evidence against him by its own independent labors, rather than by the cruel, simple [method] of compelling it from his own mouth.

— Chief Justice Warren, *Miranda v. Arizona* (1966)

Society has always paid a stiff price for law and order, and peaceful interrogation is not one of the dark moments.

— Justice Harlan, *Miranda v. Arizona* (1966)

FOR CRITICAL THINKING

1. Do you think the Fourteenth Amendment guarantees the Fifth Amendment right to remain silent against infringement by states? Explain.
2. Should the Fifth Amendment right to remain silent apply only to criminal court proceedings—or should it apply to police questioning of suspects as well? Explain.
3. Do you think that Miranda's signing of a confession, after the typed-in statement on the confession form had been read to him, amounted to his giving up his constitutional rights? Explain.
4. Do the quotes from Chief Justice Warren and Justice Harlan (at left) help you decide this case? Explain. Which of the two quotes do you think is from the majority opinion and which from a dissenting opinion? Why?
5. How do you think the Supreme Court ruled in this case?

SCHMERBER V. CALIFORNIA (1966)

Problems of "unreasonable search and seizure" sometimes overlap with those involving "self-incrimination." That has happened when law officers try to extract evidence from a person's body. The problem arose in Rochin v. California *(1952). In this case state officers, suspecting Rochin of selling narcotics, forced their way into his bedroom and spied two capsules lying on a night stand. Rochin swallowed them. The officers hurried him to a hospital where doctors extracted two morphine tablets by pumping out his stomach. The Supreme Court, however, overturned Rochin's conviction for narcotics possession because the evidence had been obtained by methods that "shocked the conscience." Two justices said that the Fifth Amendment privilege against self-incrimination applied. But the majority relied on the due process clause of the Fourteenth Amendment. Then, in 1966, came the following case.*

Sometime around midnight, Armando Schmerber and his friend walked out of a Los Angeles tavern and bowling alley where they had been drinking. They got into the car, and Schmerber roared away. Suddenly the car whipped into a skid, crossed the road, and smashed into a tree. Both Schmerber and his companion were injured.

A police officer arrived shortly after the accident. He said he smelled liquor on Schmerber's breath and saw that his eyes had a "bloodshot, watery, sort of glassy appearance." Later, at the hospital where Schmerber and his friend were taken for treatment, the investigating officer said he noticed similar symptoms of drunkenness. He placed Schmerber under arrest—informing him that he was entitled to counsel, that he could remain silent, and that anything he said could be used against him.

The officer also ordered a physician to conduct a blood test for alcohol on Schmerber. On the advice of his attorney, Schmerber refused to consent. But in spite of his refusal, the blood sample was drawn and it revealed enough alcohol in Schmerber's blood to indicate intoxication.

At Schmerber's trial in Los Angeles Municipal Court, both the officer's testimony and the chemical analysis of Schmerber's blood were introduced. Schmerber was convicted of violating that section of the California Vehicle Code that provided, "It is unlawful for any person who is under the influence of any intoxicating liquor . . . to drive a vehicle upon any highway. . . ." The crime was a misdemeanor.

Schmerber appealed his conviction. He contended that the taking of the blood sample under those circumstances and the admission of the chemical analysis as evidence denied him "due process of law" under the Fourteenth Amendment. He also claimed that these acts abridged his rights against "unreasonable search and seizure" protected by the Fourth Amendment and his privilege against "self-incrimination" protected by the Fifth Amendment. The Fourteenth Amendment, contended Schmerber, made these protections apply to the states. The Appellate Department of the California Superior Court rejected these arguments and affirmed Schmerber's conviction. The case eventually came before the U.S. Supreme Court.

FOR CRITICAL THINKING

1. In what way do you think *Rochin v. California* (1952) was like this case? In what way was it different?
2. Do you think the Fourth Amendment's ban against "unreasonable search and seizure" should apply to one's person as well as to his or her home? Why or why not?
3. Do you think that an officer investigating such a case as this should be required to go before a judge and get a search warrant before ordering that a blood sample be taken from a drunken-driving suspect? What risk would the officer run, if any, in taking the time to go before a judge? Should this matter? Explain your answer.
4. Does the quote from Justice Abe Fortas (at left) help you decide this case? Explain. Do you think it is from the majority or from a dissenting opinion? Why?
5. How do you think the Supreme Court ruled in this case?

As prosecutor, the state has no right to commit any kind of violence upon the person or to utilize the results of such [an offense], and the extraction of blood, over protests, is an act of violence.

— Justice Fortas, *Schmerber v. California* (1966)

SHEPPARD V. MAXWELL (1966)

Trial by an impartial jury is one of the most cherished tenets in our legal system. The Sixth Amendment, for example, guarantees "a speedy and public trial by an impartial jury." The long-standing issue has been, how "public"? Specifically, how far may news media go in reporting on the events and participants in a criminal trial?

This area has been strained with tension between two fundamental American principles: the right of the accused to a fair trial versus freedom of the press. The defendant claims the right of protection against harmful publicity—during both the pretrial and trial stages—that would make it impossible to find an "impartial jury" in the community. The press, on the other hand, claims that it serves the public's right to know about criminal proceedings. This helps check secret abuses of judicial power, as well as the miscarriage of justice. These two doctrines clashed head-on in the sensational case described below.

In all criminal prosecutions, the accused shall enjoy the right to a speedy and public trial, by an impartial jury. . . .

— 6th Amendment, U.S. Constitution (1791)

As Bay Village, Ohio—a quiet, middle-class suburb west of Cleveland —slept by the shores of Lake Erie, July 4, 1954, dawned with a shock. Police sped on call to the lakeside home of Dr. Sam Sheppard. In a bedroom his pregnant wife, Marilyn, lay dead in a pool of blood, the victim of a savage and brutal beating.

Almost immediately, suspicion focused on Dr. Sheppard. On July 30 he was arrested and charged with his wife's murder. The sensational case hit front pages everywhere. Television and radio commentators broadcast every detail they could get their hands on to an eager public across the nation. In a televised three-day inquest held in a school gymnasium, a coroner questioned Dr. Sheppard for more than five hours before an audience of several hundred spectators. Reporters and photographers swarmed about. When he forcibly ejected Sheppard's lawyer from the inquest, the coroner drew "cheers, hugs, and kisses from ladies in the audience." On August 17, Sheppard was indicted for first degree murder.

More than three weeks before the trial, newspapers published the names and addresses of prospective jurors. Several of them received letters and telephone calls about the case. The trial began on October 18—two weeks before "a hotly contested election" in which the trial judge and the chief prosecutor were candidates for judgeships. During the trial, reporters were allowed to move around freely in the small courtroom, "hounding" Sheppard and other participants. Twenty reporters were assigned seats at a table close enough to Sheppard and his lawyer to prevent privacy between them. Three of the four rows of benches normally available to spectators had been reserved for members of the press, radio, and television. Reporters constantly coming in and going out caused confusion and disrupted the trial. The trial judge even assigned to a broadcasting station a room next to the jury room.

From the outset, all this activity as well as the widespread publicity gave Dr. Sheppard's trial "a carnival atmosphere." Day after day, the public and jurors were treated to opinion-shaping headlines, such as "Quit Stalling and Bring Him In" . . . "Sam Declined July 4 Lie Test" . . . "Says Dr. Sam Talked Divorce" . . . "Says Marilyn Called Sam a Jekyll-Hyde." Many of the news stories included information that tended to hurt Sheppard's case but which had not been introduced at the trial. News media frequently interviewed witnesses and published their testimony even before they testified in court. Officers—as well as attorneys from both sides—"leaked" information and gossip to newspaper, radio, and television journalists.

The jury had access to all publicity given the case, although the trial judge made "suggestions" and "requests" that the jurors not expose themselves to such comments. At the very start of the proceedings as well as later, the judge announced that neither he, nor anyone else, could restrict harmful news accounts of the trial.

Several times during the trial, Sheppard filed motions for a change of venue [to move the trial to another place] and to hold the trial at a later time. Both motions were denied by the court.

On December 17, nine weeks after the trial began, the jurors began deliberation of the case. They were isolated during a five-day period but were allowed to make telephone calls to their families. On December 21, the jury brought in a verdict: guilty of second-degree murder. Sam Sheppard was sentenced to life in prison.

During a review by a federal district court, Sheppard argued that the atmosphere in Cleveland as a result of all the publicity prevented him from having a fair trial. Therefore, he said, the judge erred in denying the motions to change the place and time of the trial. Sheppard also argued that, according to state law, communication with the jury was not permitted during deliberation, except by court order. And, although no court order had been obtained, the jurors had been allowed to telephone members of their families.

The state of Ohio answered that a denial of a motion to change the place of trial was justified. The great majority of prospective jurors had said they were not and would not be subject to outside influence if accepted on the jury. Besides, argued the state, the case was almost as well-known anywhere else in the nation as in the Cleveland area. Although the telephone calls to the jurors during deliberation were unauthorized, contended the state, these amounted to mere assurances concerning the welfare of their families. And, it was argued, these calls made the jurors more conscientious in the performance of their duty. The bailiff in charge of the jurors testified that during these telephone conversations he had not overheard any remarks concerning the case or the deliberations.

The federal district court held that Sheppard had not been given a fair trial. But a U.S. Court of Appeals affirmed his earlier conviction. Then Dr. Sheppard brought his case to the U.S. Supreme Court.

FOR CRITICAL THINKING

1. Do you think that the due process clause of the Fourteenth Amendment required the trial judge to protect the defendant from harmful news stories before and during the trial? If so, how could a judge exercise such control without interfering with the freedom of the press guaranteed under the First Amendment?

2. Do you agree or disagree with the state of Ohio's argument that the telephone calls to jurors made them more conscientious in their duties? What danger, if any, was risked in allowing these telephone calls during the jury's five-day deliberation?

3. Should the trial judge have permitted the news media to interview witnesses about their testimony before they gave it in court? Why or why not?

4. Should the trial judge have tried to prevent officials and attorneys from "leaking" information about the trial to the press? Why or why not?

5. How do you think the Supreme Court ruled in this case?

BERGER V. NEW YORK (1967)

The "eavesdropper" once listened by the naked ear under the eaves of houses. At such close range, the eavesdropper had to hide constantly to prevent discovery. All that changed with the invention of the telephone. "Wiretapping"—clandestine taps, or connections, attached onto telephone lines—enabled the eavesdropper to overhear private conversations from miles away. Still, this technique was restricted, by its nature, to telephone and telegraph communications. Any such limitation, however, was destroyed by the development of modern electronic "bugs"—tiny wireless transmitters hidden in books, fountain pens, cuff links. These devices could pick up even a whisper throughout a room where they were planted.

Government officers traditionally claim the need to use eavesdropping to collect evidence in national security and organized crime cases. Such offenders are sophisticated and well equipped, so the argument goes, and it is necessary to fight fire with fire. Critics of wiretapping and bugging, however, hold that these devices pose an almost limitless threat to the cherished right of privacy. They also claim that such methods have produced very few convictions. By state and federal laws, wiretapping has been narrowly restricted in America. However, bugging—which poses a greater threat to privacy—has been generally permitted, both for official and private operators. The following is a landmark case in this area.

Bursting into a New York bar and grill, agents of the State Liquor Authority seized the owner's books and records. The owner, Ralph Pansini, complained to the district attorney's office. He said the raid was a reprisal for his failure to pay a bribe in order to get a liquor license.

The district attorney's office was not shocked by Pansini's story. It had received numerous complaints indicating that officials of the State Liquor Authority and private attorneys were involved in a racket to force applicants for liquor licenses to pay large bribes. To support his complaint, Pansini was able to supply recorded interviews between himself and, first, an employee of the Authority who advised that the "going rate" for a liquor license was $10,000, and later, a lawyer named Harry Neyer who was recommended by the employee.

A justice of the New York Supreme Court, after being advised of the recorded interviews, issued an order to install a recording device in Neyer's office for a period of sixty days. A New York statute authorized such eavesdrop orders when issued upon the "oath or affirmation of a district attorney, or of the attorney general, or of an officer above the rank of sergeant of any police department."

Based on leads obtained from the Neyer recordings, a second eavesdrop order was obtained. This permitted the installation, also for sixty days, of a listening device in the office of Harry Steinman. Then, after two weeks of eavesdropping, a key conversation was recorded between Steinman and Ralph Berger. This conversation indicated that Berger was a "go-between" in the bribery conspiracy.

The right of the people to be secure in their persons, houses, papers, and effects, against unreasonable searches and seizures, shall not be violated; and no warrants shall issue but upon probable cause, supported by oath or affirmation, and particularly describing the place to be searched, and the persons or things to be seized.

— 4th Amendment, U.S. Constitution (1791)

Berger was indicted on the charge of conspiring to bribe a public officer of the New York State Liquor Authority. The grand jury believed that Berger was doing his best to influence the Authority official to issue liquor licenses to certain clubs in New York.

At Berger's trial, portions of the recordings were played to the jury. Berger filed a motion to suppress the eavesdrop evidence, claiming that it had been obtained illegally. He said that insufficient grounds had been shown for the eavesdrop orders—which, therefore, were invalid under the Fourth Amendment (see quote at left). Also, the eavesdrops, which were of the room-type rather than the wiretap-type, were unconstitutional because they were an intrusion into private premises.

The state argued against Berger's motion to suppress the evidence. Without the evidence and leads obtained from the eavesdrops, the district attorney said he would have no information on which to prosecute Berger. Electronic eavesdropping, declared the state, is an important technique of law enforcement. Outlawing it would severely cripple the detection of crime—especially organized crime. Criminals use modern techniques to break the law; to catch them, police must also make reasonable use of modern techniques. The New York court denied Berger's motion to suppress.

Ralph Berger was convicted by the New York court on the charge of bribery. He later appealed his case to the U.S. Supreme Court.

FOR CRITICAL THINKING

1. Do you agree or disagree with Berger's argument that the eavesdrop device, planted on private premises, was an unconstitutional invasion of his privacy? Explain.
2. Do you agree or disagree with New York's argument that electronic eavesdropping is so important a technique that, without it, the police fight against modern crime would be crippled? Explain your answer.
3. How do you think the Supreme Court ruled in this case?

IN RE GAULT (1967)

In theory, juvenile courts act as guardians, in place of parents. The primary aim is to rehabilitate "delinquent" youngsters—rather than punish them along with hardened adult criminals. Twentieth-century reformers who began such courts established far fewer formal procedures than in adult criminal trials. Public trial, trial by jury—such things were not required. The juvenile judge was to hold a casual conference with offenders and their parents. Court staff specialists—doctors, psychologists, and social workers—were to help diagnose the juveniles' problems and help in their treatment.

Actual operation of the juvenile court system in America, however, has provoked serious protest. Critics point to poorly educated judges, inadequate or nonexistent staff specialists, insufficient funds, enormous case loads. They also claim that "reform schools" used in the juvenile court's rehabilitation process are little more than temporary storage bins. The following juvenile court case deals with some of those grave charges.

For a hot June morning in Gila County, Arizona, events moved swiftly. A resident named Mrs. Cook reported to the authorities that she had received an obscene telephone call. The call was traced to the neighboring home of the Gaults. The sheriff sped to the house. Here he found two teenage boys, Gerald Gault and his friend Ronald Lewis, at home alone. Mr. and Mrs. Gault were both at work. Although the sheriff took the two boys into custody, he left no notice of this at the Gault home.

Because Gerald and Ronald were only 15, they were taken to the Children's Detention Home. Young Gault was already on six months' probation for being "in the company" of a boy who had stolen a wallet from a woman's purse.

That evening Mrs. Gault learned of Gerald's whereabouts from the Lewis family and visited her son. A probation officer at the detention home told her why Gerald was being held. The officer said a hearing would be held in Juvenile Court the very next day, June 9.

The probation officer filed a formal petition against Gerald on the day of the hearing. It simply said that Gerald was under the age of 18 and, therefore, within the jurisdiction of the Juvenile Court, and that he was a "delinquent minor." The petition stated no factual basis for this conclusion, and the charge was not made known to Mr. and Mrs. Gault. No record of the proceedings was made. The judge asked questions about the phone call. But there was a conflict in the testimony. Gerald's mother recalled that he said he only dialed Mrs. Cook's number and then handed the phone to his friend Ronald—who made the lewd remarks. The probation officer, however, said he recalled that Gerald "admitted making one of these [obscene] statements."

On June 12, Gerald was released from the Children's Detention Home. No reason was given for his having been detained—or for his release. That same day, Mrs. Gault received a note signed by the probation officer. It notified her of the date and time for "further hearings on Gerald's delinquency."

At a second hearing, on June 15, there was further conflict in the testimony. Gerald's parents insisted that he merely had dialed the number and that Ronald Lewis had made the remarks. Again Mrs. Cook was not present. When Mrs. Gault asked that Mrs. Cook be brought in to court to identify which boy had made the remarks, the Juvenile Court replied that she "didn't have to be present at the hearing." At the conclusion of the hearing, the judge committed Gerald as a "juvenile delinquent" to the State Industrial School "for the period of his minority, unless sooner discharged by due process of law." This order committed Gerald Gault, age 15, to reform school for 6 years, until he was 21 years old. If Gerald had been over 18 and had been tried in a regular criminal court, his maximum penalty under Arizona law would have been a fine of $5 to $50—or imprisonment for not more than two months.

An appeal was not permitted by Arizona law in juvenile cases. So Gerald's parents filed a petition for a writ of habeas corpus—an order requiring a prisoner to be brought before a judge to determine whether he or she is being legally held. The Arizona Supreme Court referred the writ to a state Superior Court for hearing. At this hearing, the Juvenile Court judge was questioned. He testified that he had found Gerald delinquent because he was "habitually involved in immoral matters." As grounds for this conclusion, the judge declared that two years earlier Gerald had stolen a baseball glove from another companion and lied to the police about it. The judge also said that Gerald had admitted making other nuisance calls. Gerald had his own opinion of these calls: he had termed them "silly calls, or funny calls, or something like that."

When the Superior Court ruled against the Gaults on the writ of habeas corpus, they sought review by the Arizona Supreme Court. Here, the Gaults claimed that under the Juvenile Code of Arizona they had been denied "due process of law" for the following reasons: (1) they had not been given proper notice of the initial hearing or of the specific charge against their son; (2) they were not informed of their right to counsel; (3) they had not been told of their right to confront and cross-examine witnesses; (4) they had not been advised of their right against self-incrimination; (5) they had not been advised of their right to a transcript of the proceedings, and (6) they had not been told of their right to appellate review.

The Arizona Supreme Court ruled against the Gaults. It said that the informal juvenile court proceedings represented an "effort to substitute protection and guidance for punishment, to withdraw the child from criminal jurisdiction" and provide "individualized justice." Such informality, said the supreme court, "merely authorizes the [juvenile] court to disregard technical matters of procedure not affecting the fundamental right to due process of law." The state high court stated that the Arizona statute included the due-process elements to which a child was entitled in a juvenile court—and that the purpose was to "redirect and rehabilitate the child."

Then the Arizona court concluded that the Gaults had not been denied "due process" because: (1) they knew the nature of the charges against their son from the day he was taken to the detention home; (2) they had appeared at the hearings without raising any objection; (3) they knew that they could have retained counsel, called witnesses, and cross-examined the probation officer; and (4) they had been advised by the Juvenile Court judge, when Gerald had been found delinquent on the previous charge, that if the boy came before the court again, he might be committed.

After the Arizona Supreme Court ruled against the Gaults, they appealed their case to the U.S. Supreme Court.

FOR CRITICAL THINKING

1. Do you think that the witness who originally complained about the phone call, Mrs. Cook, should have been brought into juvenile court to try to identify which boy made obscene remarks? Why or why not?
2. Do you believe the special nature of juvenile court proceedings justifies overlooking some of the formal protection required in adult criminal trials? Would this special nature justify, for instance, overlooking the right to due notice of the charges? The right to counsel? The right to confront and cross-examine hostile witnesses? The right to remain silent? Give reasons for your answers.
3. Does the quote from Justice Fortas (at left) help you decide this case? Explain. Do you think it is from the majority or a dissenting opinion? Why?
4. How do you think the Supreme Court ruled in this case?

Under our Constitution, the condition of being a boy does not justify a kangaroo court.

— Justice Fortas, *In re Gault* (1967)

TERRY V. OHIO (1968)

Under the Fourth Amendment, one type of "reasonable" search and seizure is with a warrant. In this, a judicial officer must issue a search warrant—after police establish that "probable cause" exists. And the warrant must specifically describe the place to be searched and the things expected to be seized. Another type of reasonable search was approved in United States v. Rabinowitz *(1950)—one that is part of a lawful arrest. Here, the Supreme Court said, the seizure of forged postage stamps—although without a search warrant—was lawful because (1) the search was part of a legitimate arrest, (2) the search was confined to the immediate area of the arrest, and (3) the search was for evidence of a specific crime. Another problem in this Fourth Amendment area arose in the following case.*

As police detective McFadden patrolled his usual beat in downtown Cleveland for shoplifters and pickpockets, he suddenly spotted, at the corner of Huron Road and Euclid Avenue, two suspicious-looking men. They appeared to be "casing a job, a stick-up."

Officer McFadden took up a position across the street from the two men. As he watched, he saw one of the men leave the other, walk down Huron Road, pause to look in a store window, walk on a short distance, then turn around and walk back, pausing again to look in the same store window. When the walker rejoined his companion at the corner, the two conferred briefly. Then the other man took the same course down Huron Road, peered in the store window and returned to chat at the corner with the first man. Each of the men went through this routine about half a dozen times. At one of their corner conferences, they were joined by a third man, who spoke briefly with them, then departed down Euclid Avenue. The first two men resumed their pacing, peering, and conferring. After a time they left the corner together and headed down Euclid Avenue, following the route earlier taken by the third man.

Officer McFadden, a policeman with 39 years' experience, was convinced that the men were "casing" the store before a robbery. He trailed the two men down Euclid Avenue. The detective saw them meet with the third man.

Now McFadden made his move. Cautiously, he approached the three. He identified himself as a policeman and asked their names. When he received only mumbled replies, he grabbed one of the men, John Terry, spun him around so he was facing the other two and patted down the outside of his clothing. He felt a gun in Terry's overcoat pocket. Holding Terry between himself and the other two, McFadden ordered all three men into a nearby store. Inside, he told them to raise their hands and face the wall. He yelled to a store clerk to "call the wagon."

When McFadden patted the clothing of the second man, Richard Chilton, he discovered a revolver in his topcoat pocket. A similar "pat-down" of the third man, Carl Katz, however, revealed no weapon. When the police wagon arrived, the three suspects were taken to a precinct station. Here, Terry and Chilton were formally charged with carrying concealed weapons.

When Terry and Chilton were brought to trial, they filed a motion to suppress the use of the weapons as evidence. They claimed that the guns had been taken from them during an illegal arrest. The officer who stopped them did not conduct an interrogation other than to ask their names. Therefore, McFadden was attempting to arrest, not to interrogate, argued the defendants. But under the Fourth Amendment, there must be "probable cause" before an arrest can be made. And at the time, no adequate "reasonable grounds" to arrest existed. Therefore, contended Terry and Chilton, the evidence obtained during the illegal arrest should be suppressed.

The state replied that the officer suspected the men of "casing" a store for a potential daytime robbery. Therefore, it was logical for this experienced detective to presume that the men were also armed and dangerous. To ensure his own safety when he stopped them to inquire about their activities, it was valid for the officer to "frisk" the suspects for dangerous weapons. The arrest, claimed the state, did not take place until the officer ordered the men into the store, after the gun was discovered in Terry's overcoat.

Terry and Chilton were found guilty. The case eventually came before the U.S. Supreme Court, although Chilton died before the case was reviewed.

FOR CRITICAL THINKING

1. Do you think Officer McFadden had reasonable grounds to stop the three men for questioning? Why?
2. Do you think he had reasonable grounds to "frisk" them? Why?
3. Under the Fourth Amendment, must a police officer always obtain a search warrant before making a search? If yes, explain why.
4. In what ways is this case similar to *United States v. Rabinowitz* (1950)? In what ways is it different?
5. Do you think the type of "stop" procedure used by McFadden is a "seizure" within the meaning of the Fourth Amendment? Explain your answer.
6. Do you think the type of "frisk" he used is a "search" within the meaning of the Fourth Amendment? Why?
7. How do you think the Supreme Court ruled in this case?

DUNCAN V. LOUISIANA (1968)

A person accused of crime can be tried in two ways. One is a bench trial and the other, a jury trial. In the first a judge decides both questions of law and questions of fact at the trial. In the second, a jury decides the questions of fact and the judge determines which rules of law to apply to the facts of the case.

Jury trials in criminal cases existed in England for several centuries prior to the Constitution. Many experts trace them back to the Magna Charta, the basic English charter of civil liberties in 1215 A.D. In our own Bill of Rights, the Sixth Amendment to the Constitution declares: "In all criminal prosecutions, the accused shall enjoy the right to a speedy and public trial, by an impartial jury of the state and district wherein the crime shall have been committed. . . ." In addition, all state constitutions require jury trials in certain types of criminal cases. This case arose in a dispute over the demand for a jury trial.

Desegregration had brought tension to a formerly all-white high school in Plaquemines Parish, Louisiana. Racial violence had recently flared. A black teenager, Gary Duncan, was driving along Highway 23 on October 18 when he saw his two younger cousins talking to four white boys by the side of the road. He slowed down. His cousins had recently transferred to the integrated high school. And Gary worried that trouble might be brewing now.

Gary stopped the car and got out. He walked over to the six boys. What happened after that is not entirely clear. But witnesses later agreed that Gary and the white boys spoke to each other. Gary asked his cousins to get into the car with him, and they did. Then, as Gary was entering the car, a scuffle occurred. The white boys claimed that Gary slapped one of them, Herman Landry, on the elbow. Gary's cousins argued that he had not slapped Herman but merely touched him.

On Herman Landry's complaint, Gary Duncan was charged by local authorities with simple battery—a misdemeanor punishable by a fine of not more than $300 or imprisonment for not more than two years, or both. At his hearing in a state district court, Gary asked for a jury trial. His request was denied by the judge. According to the Louisiana state constitution, a trial by jury was required only in cases that involve capital punishment or hard labor. After hearing the facts in the case, the trial judge ruled that the state had proved beyond a reasonable doubt that Gary Duncan had committed simple battery. Thus convicted, Gary was sentenced to serve sixty days in the parish prison and pay a fine of $150.

Gary appealed his case to the Supreme Court of Louisiana, which denied him a review. His attorneys then appealed to the U.S. Supreme Court. The state of Louisiana argued that even if it had to grant jury trials in serious criminal cases, this was merely a petty offense of simple battery in which the defendant was sentenced to only sixty days in jail. Duncan's lawyers replied that the Fourteenth Amendment (at left) made the Sixth Amendment guarantee of trial by jury in criminal cases applicable to the states. These were their main arguments:

No state shall make or enforce any law which shall abridge the privileges or immunities of citizens of the United States; nor shall any state deprive any person of life, liberty, or property, without due process of law; nor deny to any person within its jurisdiction the equal protection of the laws.

— 14th Amendment, U.S. Constitution (1868)

1. Supreme Court doctrine in the past has held that the Fourteenth Amendment does not automatically make any of the specific guarantees of the Sixth Amendment applicable to the states. Instead, the decision to apply a specific guarantee of the Bill of Rights to state criminal proceedings has depended on whether the right is so fundamental and essential to a "fair trial" that it is incorporated in the due process clause of the Fourteenth Amendment.
2. Trial by jury was an important feature of English common

law, and was recognized by the framers of the U.S. Constitution as being an essential element of a fair trial.

3. The U.S. Supreme Court has consistently recognized trial by jury in criminal cases as a right of fundamental importance.
4. Trial by jury in criminal cases makes the individual's life and liberty safe from arbitrary official conduct by judges.
5. A jury assures humane, common-sense application of the laws. It helps soften harsh or technical application of the law that might occur in some instances through judges alone.

FOR CRITICAL THINKING

1. Would you classify this case as primarily a right to counsel case, a self-incrimination case, a search-and-seizure case, a juvenile right case, a trial by jury case, or an impartial judge case? Explain.
2. Why do you think Louisiana had a law limiting trial by jury to cases involving capital punishment and acts punishable by hard labor?
3. How would a change of procedure in this matter affect the case load in criminal courts?
4. Do you think that Gary Duncan was entitled to trial by jury given the circumstances of the case? Why or why not?
5. Do you think the Fourteenth Amendment made all aspects of the Sixth Amendment apply to the states? (Read both amendments carefully before giving your answer.) Explain.
6. How do you think the Supreme Court ruled in this case?

BIVENS V. SIX AGENTS OF THE FEDERAL BUREAU OF NARCOTICS (1971)

In what ways are citizens protected from unconstitutional searches? This had long been debated by the U.S. Supreme Court. One of the chief ways has been the "exclusionary rule." Under the principle, if a police officer uncovers damaging evidence during an unconstitutional search, the evidence can be "excluded" by defendants in their criminal trial. The rule was first applied to federal criminal trials in Weeks v. United States *(1914). In 1961, the Supreme Court applied the exclusionary rule to state criminal trials in* Mapp v. Ohio. *Ten years later came the following case.*

The morning routine of the Bivens family was suddenly shattered. Their New York City apartment was raided by six agents of the U.S. Bureau of Narcotics. They arrested Webster Bivens on alleged drug violations. They handcuffed him in front of his wife and children. And threatening to arrest the entire family, the agents searched the apartment from top to bottom. They found nothing.

Next the officers took Webster Bivens to a federal courthouse in Brooklyn. Here he was interrogated, booked, and subjected to a strip search. Webster Bivens brought suit against the agents in a federal district court. He charged them with entering and searching his apartment without a warrant and using unreasonable force in making the arrest. He also alleged that the arrest was made without probable cause. Bivens claimed to have suffered great embarrassment and mental suffering as a result of the agents' unlawful conduct. He sought $15,000 damages from each of them, charging they had violated his rights under the Fourth Amendment.

The district court dismissed Bivens' complaint on the grounds that it failed to state a "cause of action." This meant that there were no grounds for a federal remedy based upon the facts presented in the Bivens case. There was no federal law that specifically stated a person could bring action in a federal court for money damages in an unreasonable search. Until Congress passed such a law, said the court, money damage claims involving Fourth Amendment rights could not be considered.

The case eventually came before the U.S. Supreme Court. The court agreed to hear the matter because it raised some important new points. The court had established that, in a criminal case, any evidence obtained by officers of the law in violation of the Fourth Amendment could not be used at trial against the defendant. Therefore, even if the agents had found evidence damaging to Bivens, they could not have presented it because of the way they entered and searched the apartment. In addition, any person who was harmed by another had a right in state court to file a civil suit for damages against the wrongdoer.

The Bivens case raised these issues: (1) Could a person who suffered harm as a result of loss of Fourth Amendment rights sue federal agents who, while performing their duties, caused such harm? (2) Could such a suit be tried in a federal court?

Webster Bivens claimed "yes" on both issues. The federal agents claimed immunity from prosecution based upon a valid exercise of federal power. They argued that state courts had no right to entertain suits against them in the exercise of their duties as agents of the federal government. Moreover, the agents maintained that before such suits could be brought against them in a federal court, Congress would have to pass specific legislation that dealt with violation of Fourth Amendment rights. Attorneys for Webster Bivens answered that:

1. The possibility of a federal damage claim for an unconstitutional search and seizure has been recognized in a number of earlier Supreme Court cases.
2. A new law does not have to be passed by Congress. The law already exists that would allow for redress of damages to Bivens. That law is the Fourth Amendment to the Constitution. And the Constitution is meant to be respected as the highest law in the land by the courts. Federal courts do have the power to award damages for violation of constitutionally protected interests.

FOR CRITICAL THINKING

1. Would you classify this case as primarily a right to counsel case, a self-incrimination case, a search and seizure case, a juvenile

The right of the people to be secure in their persons, houses, papers, and effects, against unreasonable searches and seizures, shall not be violated; and no warrants shall issue but upon probable cause, supported by oath or affirmation, and particularly describing the place to be searched, and the persons or things to be seized.

— 4th Amendment, U.S. Constitution (1791)

rights case, a trial by jury case, or an impartial judge case? Explain your answer.

2. What was the main issue in this case?

3. Why do you think attorneys for Webster Bivens insisted upon taking this case to a federal court? Would it matter that Bivens would be generally entitled to damages for mental and physical stress for such a search under New York State law? Why?

4. In what way, if any, does the Fourth Amendment (see quote at left) apply to this case?

5. If you were called on to argue this case, what arguments would you offer on behalf of Bivens? On behalf of the six agents?

6. How do you think the Supreme Court ruled in this case?

GREGG V. GEORGIA (1976)

Excessive bail shall not be required, nor excessive fines imposed, nor cruel and unusual punishments inflicted.

— 5th Amendment, U.S. Constitution (1791)

The Bill of Rights was written, in part, to protect citizens from the kinds of inhumane tortures and painful executions that had been prevalent in England during the reign of King James II. Hence, the Eighth Amendment barred the federal government from inflicting "cruel or unusual" punishments on any individual convicted of a crime (see quote at left). At that time, 1791, death was not considered a cruel and unusual punishment for crimes such as murder, treason, and rape.

By the mid-twentieth century, however, many people began to change their minds about the use of the death penalty. In Trop v. Dulles *(1958), the U.S. Supreme Court said the meaning of "cruel and unusual" punishment was tied to the American public's "evolving standards of decency." After that, many states refused to inflict the punishment of death for any crime. Then, the Supreme Court, in* Furman v. Georgia *(1972), invalidated all existing state and federal death penalty laws, though not the death penalty itself. It was in this social climate that the following pivotal case arose three years later.*

In a grisly murder along a Georgia highway in 1973, a young hitchhiker named Troy Leon Gregg killed two men who had given him a ride. According to District Attorney Bryant Huff, who prosecuted the case, Gregg wanted to steal the victims' car and their money—about $400. To do this, Gregg shot the two after they stopped to rest by the roadside. He then walked to the ditch where the bodies had fallen and fired a bullet into the skull of each man.

At his trial, Gregg claimed that he shot the two men in self-defense. After telling him they had committed a crime, they grew afraid that he might go to the police, and so, said Gregg, they attacked him. The jury refused to believe Gregg's story, and returned a verdict of guilty. Huff then asked for the death penalty. "If anybody is ever deserving of the death penalty," he said, "Gregg would be."

Under Georgia law, the case had to go before a second jury. That jury, after considering all the circumstances of the case, agreed with Huff's recommendation. There followed an automatic review process in which the Georgia Supreme Court compared the case with others to determine whether the death sentence was appropriate. The state court recommended the death penalty too.

The Georgia law was written following the Supreme Court decision in *Furman v. Georgia* (1972). In that case the Court ruled that the death penalty violated the Eighth Amendment's ban on cruel and unusual punishment. It cited the arbitrary and "freakish" way in which some defendants were sentenced to die and others were allowed to live. Georgia and several other states quickly passed new laws that provided juries and judges with more information and guidance before asking for the death penalty. Jimmy Carter, governor at the time, signed Georgia's death penalty into law in 1973.

Gregg's lawyers asked that the U.S. Supreme Court review his case. They argued that the death penalty remained excessively cruel. One main objective of punishment was to rehabilitate, or change, criminals so that they could return to their communties as productive citizens. Certainly the death penalty could not accomplish this. In Georgia, imprisonment was an available alternative for the crime committed by the petitioner.

The defendant also charged that there was no conclusive proof that the death penalty was an effective deterrent to crime. Finally, he argued, the killing of people by the state is barbaric, a relic of the past that should have no place in civilized society.

Georgia answered that the wording of the Constitution and previous Supreme Court decisions established that the death penalty was constitutional. The state strongly argued that the death penalty was a deterrent to crime. While other penalties such as life imprisonment were available for serious crimes, this did not mean that the death penalty was unnecessary. It simply meant that each case should be considered according to its own special circumstances. States should have the right to determine their own "standards of decency," and juries should be able to recommend death if the situation required it.

FOR CRITICAL THINKING

1. Do you think society's attitudes about the death penalty have changed in recent years? If so, how?
2. How would you define the term "cruel and unusual?" Do you think the death penalty is "cruel and unusual" in our present society? Why?
3. What do you think the goals of our nation's criminal justice system should be? What kinds of punishments would achieve those goals?
4. Does the quote from Justice Stewart (left) help you decide this case? Explain. Do you think it is from a majority or a dissenting opinion? Why?
5. How do you think the Supreme Court ruled in this case?

Legislative measures adopted by the people's chosen representatives weigh heavily in ascertaining contemporary standards of decency.

— Justice Stewart, *Gregg v. Georgia* (1976)

IMMIGRATION AND NATURALIZATION SERVICE V. LOPEZ-MENDOZA (1984)

Under the "exclusionary rule," illegally obtained evidence violates the Fourth Amendment's protection against unreasonable search and seizure. In Weeks v. United States *(1914) the Supreme Court overturned the conviction of Fremont Weeks—not because he was innocent, but because the evidence used to convict him had been obtained without a warrant.*

Over the years, many people have criticized the exclusionary rule. They claim that because of technicalities, criminals often are allowed to go free. Surely, they say, the framers of the Constitution did not intend for thieves and murderers to go unpunished. In response to these criticisms, the Court in the 1970's and 1980's began to pull back from total reliance on the exclusionary rule. In Nix v. Williams *(1984) the Court said the illegally obtained evidence may be used if it would "inevitably" have been discovered by legal means. In that same year, the Court heard the case of* United States v. Leon. *The police in that case had used a warrant containing legal errors. But the Court ruled that since the police had acted in "good faith" and had good reason to believe their search was legal, the evidence could be used. Another challenge to the exclusionary rule came in the following case.*

Adan Lopez-Mendoza worked at an auto repair shop in San Mateo, California. One day in 1977 an agent from the Immigration and Naturalization Service (INS) entered the shop. Lopez-Mendoza's boss asked that the INS agent not talk to any of the employees during work hours. The agent agreed, but then diverted the shop owner's attention while a second agent approached Lopez-Mendoza. The Mexican admitted he was an illegal alien and was arrested.

Lopez-Mendoza challenged a subsequent deportation order on the grounds that the arrest was illegal. The circuit court of appeals agreed with him, saying that a person accused of being in this country illegally may not be deported based on evidence that was illegally obtained. The decision, the appeals court went on to point out, would only affect a tiny number of cases. "Only [a] fraction of the illegal alien population will mount challenges based on the exclusionary rule," the court said, noting that most illegal immigrants were likely to be poor, uneducated, and unable to speak English. "The small number who do so successfully will not [greatly] increase the number of illegal aliens in our midst." In fact, in the 20th century only two immigration cases had been heard in which the exclusionary rule was invoked.

The Reagan administration took the case to the Supreme Court. It said that extending exclusionary rule protection to alleged illegal aliens would harm the government's efforts in stemming illegal immigration. Such protection, the Justice Department said, "threatens mortal injury to the enforcement of our immigration laws and may create a new class of aliens whose only . . . right to U.S. residency is a judge's opinion suppressing evidence." It noted that in 1983 more than one million illegal aliens were arrested. How could INS officers be expected to compile elaborate written reports detailing the circumstances of every arrest where there were so many?

Important as it is to protect the Fourth Amendment rights of all persons [against unreasonable search and seizure], there is no convincing indication that application of the exclusionary rule in civil deportation proceedings will contribute materially to that end.

— Justice O'Connor, *INS v. Lopez-Mendoza* (1984)

FOR CRITICAL THINKING

1. What is the exclusionary rule? What is a major criticism of it?
2. How did the exclusionary rule apply to this case?
3. Do you think aliens who enter this country illegally should be granted the same Fourth Amendment rights as American citizens? Why or why not?
4. Does the quote from Justice O'Connor (left) help you decide this case? Explain. Do you think it is from a majority or dissenting opinion? Why?
5. How do you think the Supreme Court ruled in this case?

NEW JERSEY V. T.L.O. (1985)

*The question of what is a reasonable search continues to confront the Supreme Court. In general, the Court has ruled that a search without a warrant is reasonable if police have good reason to believe a suspect will harm others, escape, or destroy evidence. In addition, inspectors at airports or border crossings do not need warrants to search for weapons or drugs. The Court also ruled, in 1985, that the Environmental Protection Agency could fly over private property to search for toxic waste dumps (*Dow Chemical Co. v. EPA.*)*

In that same year the following case, involving school administrators and students, came before the Court. For the first time, the justices dealt with the rights of public school students to be free from unreasonable searches and seizures.

T.L.O., a 14-year-old freshman, had broken the rules of her New Jersey high school. A teacher had found her smoking in the school bathroom and had taken her to the principal's office. T.L.O. denied that she had been smoking. She said she did not smoke at all.

The Vice Principal, who was questioning T.L.O., then opened her purse and found a pack of cigarettes. As he rummaged through her purse, he also noticed cigarette papers used in smoking marijuana. He then looked further and found some marijuana. He also found a substantial sum of cash, a list of students said to owe T.L.O. money, and letters suggesting that T.L.O. was a drug dealer. On this evidence, T.L.O. was brought before the Juvenile Court, which decided that she was a drug dealer and a juvenile delinquent.

T.L.O. appealed on the grounds that in searching her purse the Vice Principal had violated her Fourth Amendment rights. She claimed that the evidence on which she was convicted was illegally seized and should not have been used against her. As far as the Vice Principal knew, no crime was involved, only a school rule. Further, the possession of cigarettes in her purse in no way proved that she was smoking in the lavoratory. The New Jersey Supreme Court ruled in her favor. The prosecutor then took the case to the U.S. Supreme Court.

FOR CRITICAL THINKING

1. Would you classify this case primarily as a right to counsel case, a self-incrimination case, a search-and-seizure case, a juvenile right case, a trial by jury case, or an impartial judge case? Explain.
2. Do you think that the fact T.L.O. had cigarettes in her purse proved she was a smoker? Give reasons for your answer.
3. Do you think school officials should have the right to search purses? What about lockers? Explain your answer.
4. How do you think the Supreme Court ruled in this case?

EXPLORING THE MAIN IDEAS

WHAT DO YOU THINK

1. Which of the cases in this chapter concern the right to counsel? Which, the right to remain silent? Which, the right to confront and cross-examine hostile witnesses? Which cases concern questions of search and seizure? Which concern jury qualifications? Which amendments in the Bill of Rights protect these rights in federal criminal cases? Which amendment protects these rights in state criminal cases?
2. Do you think the threat of death acts as a deterrent to certain crimes? Why or why not?
3. What is your opinion of the exclusionary rule?

THINGS TO DO

1. Appoint a class fact-finding committee to investigate and report to the class on how jury members are selected in your community. If possible, interview people who have sat on a jury and determine what questions they were asked before they were chosen.
2. Appoint another class committee to obtain from your police department a ''Miranda card''—or the formal statement read by an arresting police officer to a suspect.
3. Attend a criminal trial at a local courthouse. Write a report on your impressions, indicating whether you think the procedures you learned about in this chapter were followed both before and during the trial.

Illustration Review

Now that you have finished this chapter's cases, re-analyze the pictures on pages 100–101. Which cases relate to which pictures? In what ways, if any, would your answers to the questions in ''Illustration Analysis'' at the beginning of the chapter now change? In what ways if any, would your answers remain the same?

Mock Trial

This mock trial has been designed especially for classroom use. It has all the drama of a real trial. Yet its steps are so simple that most cases can be completed in one class period.

The mock trial follows the proceedings of a trial at its lowest court level. Most of the cases in this book can be adapted to this method by imagining what may have taken place at the first trial—that is, before the case was appealed to a higher court.

PARTICIPANTS AND SCRIPTS

A few days before the trial, the following participants are chosen: (a) judge; (b) plaintiff (or, in a criminal case, the victim-complaintant if one is needed); (c) plaintiff's attorney (prosecuting attorney in a criminal trial); (d) witnesses for the plaintiff (or prosecution); (e) defendant; (f) defendant's attorney; (g) witnesses for the defendant; (h) panel of jurors; (i) clerk; (j) court reporter; and (k) bailiff. The jury normally has twelve members, but it may have as few as six jurors chosen by lot. Or the teacher may select them. In large classes, alternates for each role should be picked. This will avoid a delay on the day of the trial because of absentees.

Duties of Participants

Although you are closely imitating an actual trial, remember that this is primarily an exercise in critical thinking—to help you make decisions on your feet. Student attorneys will want to make the most persuasive case possible by questioning the various witnesses. Jurors will be weighing evidence and spotting weak points in testimonies. Witnesses will be fielding unexpected questions during cross-examination.

All participants should learn their roles well—as described below, in a general way, and later in the section entitled "Conduct of the Trial." But they should not be such sticklers for form that they forget to take advantage of forceful reasoning, quick thinking, and imagination.

Judge. This official bears the heaviest responsibility in the classroom. The judge must conduct the trial in an orderly and dignified manner, making sure that both sides have a fair chance to present their cases. And the judge must keep the trial moving briskly toward conclusion within an hour. The judge should not interrupt or dominate the proceedings in a way that overshadows the attorneys. But he or she must insist that they stick to fair rules. After both attorneys have made their closing arguments, the judge instructs the jury on what principles of law apply to the facts they have heard.

Plaintiff's Attorney. In this key role, the student must make a strong case against the defendant. The plaintiff's attorney must present enough evidence to persuade the jury to deliver a verdict against the defendant. His or her job consists of four main parts: (a) opening statement to the jury; (b) direct examination of his or her witnesses; (c) cross-examination of the witnesses of the other party; and (d) closing arguments.

Defendant's Attorney. The student in this equally vital role must show that the plaintiff's attorney did not present enough evidence to justify a verdict against the defendant. This can be done by persuading the jury that the plaintiff's evidence is unreliable, that it doesn't make sense, or that some of the witnesses disagree with each other. The defense attorney's job consists of the same parts as that of the plaintiff's attorney.

Witnesses. In an actual trial, witnesses tell the jury what they believe to be the facts. They describe what they actually saw and heard. In a mock trial, however, witnesses tell the jury the facts they recall from having read a written script. They receive this script several days before the trial. While on the witness stand, they must stick closely to the facts of their script. Occasionally, when asked on cross-examination, they may supply missing details that interpret the facts given in the script. But they may not contradict the information supplied in the script. They may not take the script with them to the stand. Therefore, they must be very familiar with the facts they can use in their testimony.

Each of the plaintiff's witnesses testifies in turn, followed by each of the defendant's witnesses. Both attorneys may ask each witness questions. A witness for the plaintiff is questioned first by the plaintiff's attorney. This is called "direct examination." Following this, the same witness undergoes "cross-examination" by the defendant's attorney. A witness for the defense first undergoes direct examination by the defendant's attorney, then cross-examination by the plaintiff's attorney.

Jury. While witnesses are being questioned, members of the jury listen closely to everything that is said. Each juror decides whether a witness's story makes sense and whether it fits with the stories of other witnesses. If two or more stories seem to conflict, a juror should consider this when reaching a decision. Jury members should also listen carefully to the instructions of the judge.

Clerk of the Court. This student (and his or her assistants) helps the teacher prepare copies of the witnesses' scripts. On the day of the trial, the clerk arranges the courtroom. The clerk also brings a watch to the trial and helps enforce time limits. The clerk opens the court session and swears in the jury.

Court Reporter. In an actual trial the reporter makes the official word-for-word transcript of all that is said and done during the proceedings. However, in a mock trial the student need only take notes of the highlights of the trial. The teacher may also request the reporter to take notes on the performance of the various participants to be used later as a springboard for evaluation in classroom discussion.

Bailiff. This student has charge of the prisoner (that is, the defendant in a criminal trial). The bailiff sees that the jurors are not interrupted during their deliberation. And, at the direction of the judge, the bailiff maintains order and delivers any written messages during the trial.

Preparation of the Scripts

With the help of the clerk and any assistant clerks, the teacher prepares the scripts for the witnesses. Normally these can be adapted from the actual cases provided in this book. After presenting several mock trials, however, teacher and student script writers may wish to make up their own legal case and develop their own scripts from this.

The teacher should check each script before the trial for sufficient detail. The clerk should then make sure both attorneys receive copies of all the scripts before the trial. From the "facts" given in the scripts, the attorneys must write the questions they will ask each witness.

Scripts should be short factual statements written in the first person. They should be based on the facts of the case as reported in this textbook. Where necessary, fictionalized details may be supplied. For some cases, script writers may wish to refer to the complete court record. U.S. Supreme Court cases can be found in the United States Reports, published by the U.S. Government Printing Office.

CONDUCT OF THE TRIAL

Since the purpose of this mock trial is to present evidence and weigh conflicting evidence, participants will want to stress their roles as opponents or as decision makers. They should not get bogged down with the mechanics of procedure or with unnecessary details.

Opening of the Court

The clerk of the court rises and says in a loud clear voice: "The Court of (*give city or state*) is now open and in session, the Honorable Judge (*give name of student judge*) presiding. All persons having business before the court come to order." When order is achieved, the clerk says: "The Case of (*give name of plaintiff or the city or state prosecuting* versus (*give name of defendant*)." After a slight pause, the clerk asks: "Is the plaintiff ready?"

Plaintiff's attorney: "The plaintiff is ready."

Clerk: "Is the defendant ready?"

COURTROOM

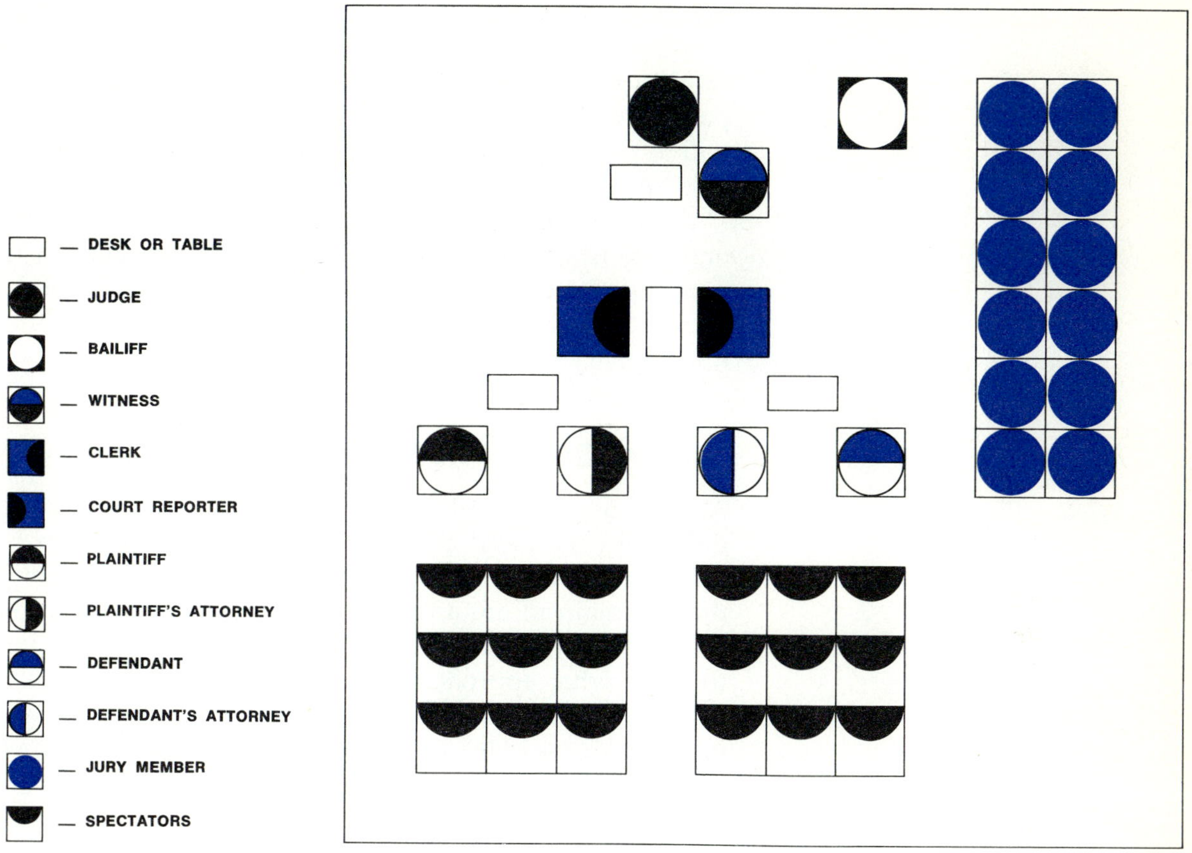

Defendant's attorney: "The defendant is ready."
Clerk: "Your Honor, may the jury be brought in?"
Judge: "Proceed with the trial of the case."

Swearing in the Jury

The clerk now directs the jury members to the seats arranged for them. When they are seated, the clerk says to them:

"The jurors will rise, raise your right hands and be sworn in. Do you solemnly swear that you will well and truly try the issues now to be given you? That you will speak nothing to anyone of the business or matters you have at hand, but among yourselves . . . nor will you suffer anyone to speak to you about the same, but in court . . . and when you are agreed upon any verdict, you will keep it secret until you deliver it up in court? Do you all so swear?"

Jurors answer together "I do."

Opening Statement By Plaintiff's Attorney

After the jury is sworn in, the plaintiff's attorney rises and makes an opening statement. Observing a five-minute time limit, the plaintiff's attorney describes the case to the jurors and gives them a summary of the essential facts. With this outline in mind, the jurors can then see how each piece of evidence presented by the witnesses relates to the plaintiff's overall argument. The plaintiff's attorney does not try to interpret what the law means in this particular case or try to predict what the opponent's argument will be. On the other side, neither can the defense attorney make objections to the opening statement of the plaintiff's attorney.

The plaintiff's attorney includes in the opening statement the name of the case, his or her own name, the client's name, the name of the defendant and the attorney's name, and the facts that led to the lawsuit. The plaintiff's attorney should avoid unnecessary detail.

Opening Statement By Defendant's Attorney

As soon as the plaintiff's attorney is finished, the attorney for the defendant rises and addresses the court, gives his or her name, and delivers a five-minute opening statement. The aim is to deny that the plaintiff has a valid case and to summarize the facts from the standpoint of the defendant. The defendant's attorney tells the jury what approach the defense will take—that is, what its testimony will show and how certain facts tend to weaken the plaintiff's case. He or she should not repeat facts which are undisputed, nor give a run-down of what each witness will say.

Direct Examination of Witnesses

Now presentation of the evidence begins, with the plaintiff's side first. The plaintiff's attorney calls each of the plaintiff's witnesses to the stand. They testify in the order in which the plaintiff's side wishes to build its case.

Each witness is sworn in by the clerk. Witnesses place their left hand on the Bible, raise their right hand, and answers "I do" to the following oath: "Do you swear to tell the whole truth and nothing but the truth in this case, únder penalty of perjury, so help you, God?" [Perjury is lying under oath—a criminal offense.]

The plaintiff's attorney begins the direct examination of the witnesses. The attorney bases his or her questions on the "facts" each witness has been given in his or her script. The attorney tries to present the witnesses to best advantage, to establish their trustworthiness, to bring out the facts of the case with clarity, and—in short—to convince the jury of the soundness of the plaintiff's case. On direct examination, an attorney may not ask leading questions—that is, ones worded so as to suggest the answers desired from the witness. When this occurs, the opposing lawyer may object. For example, an attorney may not ask a witness: "You then proceeded to tell the defendant to put away the gun, didn't you?" The opposing attorney should then say to the judge: "I object, on the grounds that the question is leading and suggestive as to answer." Suppose, however, a witness's memory fails during direct examination. In that case, the attorney may use the witness's script to help him or her remember.

The attorney on direct examination should ask friendly simple questions that give each witness a chance to tell the facts about the case. The attorney should have a good idea as to how his or her witness will answer each question. Many skilled lawyers write down in advance every question they intend to ask. The sequence of questions should build to an effective climax.

After completing the direct examination of a witness, the plaintiff's attorney turns to the defense attorney and says: "You may cross-examine." The lawyer for the defendant may then accept or decline the right to cross-examine the witness.

After the plaintiff's witnesses have all undergone both direct and cross-examination, the defense attorney begins to call the defense witnesses to the stand. After the direct examination of each defense witness is completed, the plaintiff's attorney may cross-examine them.

Cross-Examination of Witnesses

An attorney's aim in cross-examination is to get admissions from an opposing witness that will belp his or her own client's case. The lawyer may also be able to show that witnesses are unreliable or confused or that they lied during testimony.

Before the trial, each lawyer should carefully study the witnesses's scripts. Then if a witness strays markedly from the script during direct examination, the opposing attorney can try to trap the witness during cross-examination. To accomplish this, the lawyer reads the conflicting part of the witness's script to the jury. The lawyer then asks the witness if these were his or her words given in the "pretrial statement." The witness must answer "Yes." The attorney may then trap the witness by saying: "Were you lying then or are you lying now?"

During direct examination, the opposing attorney should listen carefully and take notes. If the witness gives testimony that does not make sense, the cross-examiner should ask for an explanation. If the witness gives only part of what he or she is supposed to know about certain facts, the cross-examiner may ask the witness questions that bring out the rest of the testimony.

The attorney should ask narrow, leading questions during cross-examination. The attorney can let a witness ramble, then ask: "Which question are you answering now?"

But the lawyer should never follow a question with "Why?" This would give a well-prepared witness the chance to give a damaging answer. Cross-examiners should also avoid questions for which they do not know the kinds of answers they will receive. They may try to expose lack of sincerity in a witness. But an attorney should avoid insulting or browbeating the witness—or asking confusing, double questions such as: "The defendant was there, wasn't she? What did she say?" A good judge will not permit either tactic and will make the attorney rephrase such questions.

Closing Arguments

After all defense witnesses have undergone direct and cross-examination, the attorneys for both sides present their closing arguments to the jury. Both attorneys have five minutes to summarize the points made in testimony that help their cases. The defendant's attorney gives the closing argument first. Then comes the plaintiff's attorney. The lawyers should not assume that the jury has understood all the testimony. Jurors have heard many witnesses give many statements, some of them contradictory. Each lawyer should use this chance to pull together all the parts of his or her argument as clearly as possible.

Instruction and Verdict

After closing arguments for both sides are finished, the clerk announces: "The court will now charge the jury." The judge then gives instructions to the jurors, telling them what principles of law apply to the case. For the mock trial, the student judge may write his or her instructions to the jury in advance. However, the student judge should be careful to avoid revealing the true outcome of the real case.

When the judge completes the charge, he or she announces: "Ladies and gentlemen of the jury, you may now retire and deliberate on the verdict." Instead of retiring, however, as in an actual trial, the jury should discuss the case out loud and reach its decision in front of the class. (Before discussing the case, the jury should quickly choose a foreman to act as chairman of the discussion as well as the representative of the jury to the court.) In an actual trial the vote would have to be unanimous for either side. But here, if the jury cannot reach such a verdict, a majority vote will decide the outcome. If time is short, the jury's deliberation and verdict may be postponed until the next class period.

When the jury has reached its verdict, the clerk of the court asks: "Ladies and gentlemen of the jury, have you arrived at a verdict?"

The foreman replies: "We have," and tells the court in a loud clear voice what the verdict is. The foreman may say, for example: "We the jury find for the plaintiff." Or, in a criminal case, the foreman may say: "We the jury find the defendant guilty [or not guilty]."

After the verdict, the judge (or the teacher) may lead the rest of the class in a discussion of the trial, evaluating the performances of the participants.

SAMPLE SCRIPTS FOR

The Capitol Hill Case

This hypothetical case is based on *Edwards v. South Carolina,* an actual case described in the Introduction of this book, beginning on page 1. As part of the preparation for the mock trial, all participants should review the facts of that case. Some of the information presented in these scripts is fictionalized, or made up, to supply details not given in the case study.

Presented here are examples of the kinds of scripts prepared for the witnesses, the attorneys, and the judge in a mock trial. (Using the instructions for a mock trial, which precede these sample scripts, the student judge, clerk, and foreman of the jury may, in addition, want to write out and memorize their standing lines for the conduct of any trial.)

Normally, each witness would see only his or her own script. Both attorneys, however, receive copies of all the witnesses' scripts. From these, they write the questions they will ask during examination of each witness.

Each attorney may present his or her witnesses in the order below or in any order. Attorneys should be careful to ask a witness only those questions which can be answered from the script. Witnesses, of course, do not recite their scripts word-for-word on the witness stand. Nevertheless, they must be familiar with their story in order to answer the attorneys' questions accurately.

There is no "correct" verdict in a mock trial. Script writers should not feel they are recreating an actual case exactly—nor should a student jury have to reach the same decision as the U.S. Supreme Court. Evidence presented in a mock trial will vary in different classes. Members of the jury should carefully weigh the evidence and independently reach their own decisions.

WITNESSES FOR THE STATE

Mayor Leonard

I am Mrs. Donna Leonard, the mayor of Emerson City. I've been mayor here for twelve years. And not once in all that time did we ever have any trouble in our city—not until now, anyway.

I first heard of the plans for the march when Reverend Arthur Davis applied for a permit at my office. The purpose, as stated on the request, was to "peacefully express their complaints about the laws of this state that bar black privileges." I didn't know what kind of "privileges" they meant, and I wasn't sure what they were trying to do.

Our chief of police, Louis Warren, and I discussed the problem of maintaining order for such a large gathering. The students wanted to hold the demonstration on the grounds of the state house—an area the size of two city blocks. These grounds are open to the general public. Captain Warren said he could have a number of his officers posted throughout the area. He and I finally agreed to grant the permit. But just to make sure there would be no trouble, I requested additional help from the state highway patrol.

On May 2, I arrived at the state house around 9:00 A.M. A few of the legislators were just driving into the parking lot. Everything was normal.

The marchers arrived about noon. There must've been about 300 of them. As they approached the grounds, I could sense their excitement. They were attracting a large crowd of onlookers right from the beginning. I watched the large crowds uneasily. I spotted several potential troublemakers among the spectators. But no one was actually causing a disturbance.

There must have been 1,000 onlookers in all. In some places people completely blocked the sidewalks. Pedestrians found it impossible to pass through the crowds. Traffic on the streets came to a standstill. I could see that a dangerous situation was quickly building up.

I conferred with Captain Warren. We decided to act before trouble broke out and people got hurt. The captain told Reverend Davis to disperse his group peacefully.

But the group simply ignored the order. They were extremely arrogant. They sang boisterously, clapping their hands and stamping their feet as loudly as they could. The march had clearly turned into a noisy, disorderly demonstration. We had no choice but to arrest them for disturbing the peace.

Chief Warren

My name is Louis Warren. I am chief of police in Emerson City. The mayor came to me when she received a request from Reverend Davis to hold a large demonstration. That was on April 24. With enough of my men on the scene, I thought we could maintain peace. The marchers did have the right to express their views, I felt.

On the morning set for the march, I had a dozen of my best officers stationed on the state house grounds. I stayed in the "horse-shoe" area—the section by the circular driveway and parking lot. My officers, scattered throughout the grounds, were to report any signs of a disturbance. In addition, there were about ten other officers, but these were not under my authority.

I received no word of trouble as the students marched toward the state house. They entered the grounds of the state house in small orderly groups. Many carried signs. The students attracted large crowds of onlookers, and the area started filling up quickly.

I soon got word that traffic at the corner of Main and Fifth streets was getting somewhat congested. I sent one of my officers to that intersection to keep the cars moving. At this time, I could have requested additional help, but I felt there was no need. There was no sign of violence.

After a half hour, though, traffic became totally blocked. I estimate that there were close to 1,000 people in the area. Cars were unable to enter or leave the parking area inside the state house grounds. It was then that Mayor Leonard approached me and ordered that I disperse the demonstrators.

I told Reverend Davis that he had fifteen minutes to send his people home. But I could tell immediately that he had no intention of trying to end the demonstration. In defiance of my order, he moved from group to group, urging the kids to remain where they were. They all sang "We Shall Overcome" and the "Star-Spangled Banner." Davis then deliverd a fiery speech that worked the demonstrators into a frenzy.

I was sure an outbreak of violence could occur at any moment. None of our officers spotted any weapons. But I could just feel violence in the air. After fifteen minutes, the demonstrators were still shouting and stamping their feet. I gave the signal to move in and arrest them.

My officers moved among the demonstrators quietly and efficiently and peacefully. They used no weapons or violence on those protesters—even though some of them called us names and spat on us. Our officers had to use a little self-defense to keep from getting slugged by some protesters. But they used no violence in making arrests.

Miss Marks, a Passerby

My name is Joan Marks. On May 2, I was doing some shopping near the state house when I got caught in the midst of a mob of people. They had stopped to watch some sort of huge demonstration. I could not seem to find my way out of the crowd. They were pushing this way and that. Before I knew it, I too was on the grounds of the state house.

I saw a large group of youngsters and the large signs they were waving in the air. One boldly lettered sign read "YOU MAY JAIL OUR BODIES BUT NOT OUR SOULS." There was a feeling of tension in the air I could almost touch. I caught a glimpse of one man in the crowd with a pistol sticking out of his hip pocket. It was as if the marchers wanted to cause trouble.

Then I heard them all start singing and shouting. Some of them were dancing wildly. I was sure they were trying to get arrested. But I was relieved to see how effectively our police moved in and subdued them.

WITNESSES FOR THE DEFENSE

Reverend Davis

My name is Arthur Davis. I'm the minister at the Twelfth Baptist Church in Emerson City. Many of our young people have expressed deep concern for the way blacks are treated in this state. We wanted to make the pubic aware of the injustices of our laws. After much discussion, we decided to organize a peaceful march to the state house grounds. Since the legislature would be in session, we thought we could also carry our grievances to the state representatives.

I applied for a parade permit on April 20. Two weeks passed. Finally, on May 1, we were granted the permit for the following day. Even at short notice, though, the young people were able to round up many of their friends to join us.

Everyone met at the church on the morning of the march. There were nearly 200 high school and college students—all of them eager and brave. We discussed together our plans for the day. Everyone agreed we would walk quietly and orderly.

The state house grounds are less than a mile from the church. Even so, I gave careful instructions to march in single file so we wouldn't block traffic. As the students filed out of the church, I divided them into small groups of fifteen. Then in each group, I made one student responsible for making sure everyone followed instructions.

We started marching to the state house shortly before noon. We walked peacefully. We did not block traffic—neither on the sidewalks nor in crossing the streets. Many of the other people on the streets did stop to read our signs. But no one was hostile toward us. No one threatened us.

Several police officers met us at the entrance to the state house grounds. They told us we could march in the area as long as we were peaceful. We marched quietly in single file. A crowd of about 300 spectators gathered. They apparently wanted to find out what was going on. We were glad to see them. That was part of our purpose. We hoped the legislators would also see our protest.

Then, apparently for no reason, the chief of police approached me. He demanded that we break up and go away. He said something about wanting to protect us from the huge crowd of spectators—that he didn't want us to get hurt.

I couldn't see why he was trying to disperse us. The crowd was calm. We were not unruly. But the chief told me if we didn't leave within fifteen minutes, he would arrest us for breach of peace. I knew we had the right to freedom of speech and assembly. I told the students we did not have to leave. We began singing hymns. We wanted to show we weren't afraid and that we were not going to give up our constitutional rights.

Then we were arrested. There must've been about fifty officers that moved in on us. They were poking us with their clubs even though none of our people raised a finger against them. And they called us names.

Miss Robinson, a March Leader

My name is Cora Robinson. I am a college sophomore at State Teachers A. & M., and I have been a member of the Twelfth Baptist Church for five years.

As a black American, I have personally experienced a great deal of discrimination because of my race. Many of us in the Twelfth Baptist Church have discussed this problem. We all shared a deep feeling that we had to do something about the mistreatment of minorities in our state. We decided to march to the state house to make our grievances known.

For most of us, this was our first demonstration. We were all excited—especially the younger ones. When we finally got our permit, we had only a day to get organized. We stayed up late that night making large posters to carry.

The big day finally came. I helped Reverend Davis get everyone organized before we started. We wanted everything to run smoothly. We didn't want any trouble. But since we had the permit, we didn't expect any.

We marched peacefully to the state house. As we entered the grounds, several police officers met us. I noticed a few others stationed at various points throughout the two-block area.

Silently, we walked through the grounds. Then after a half-hour, I saw the police chief approach Reverend Davis. I couldn't hear what they said to each other, but I could tell Reverend Davis was getting angry. He came to each of us group leaders and said we didn't have to leave. I knew then that the cops were threatening us. They didn't want us to publicize the truth—the truth about the unfair laws in this state. We started to sing to give ourselves courage. It was then that the cops moved in and arrested us—just because we were expressing our views and they didn't like it. I told one of those cops to keep his hands off me. Then he clobbered me.

Mr. Hamilton, a Lawyer

My name is Lester Hamilton. I am a lawyer with the firm of Hamilton and Sloane. On May 2, I had some business at the state house. I was hurrying to make a 1:00 P.M. appointment when I ran into a huge crowd of people.

My curiosity was aroused, so I elbowed my way through the throngs of people. I finally got close enough to see more than 100 young demonstrators. They were carrying placards as they walked in pairs through the grounds. They looked neat and well dressed to me. One sign read "I AM PROUD TO BE BLACK." Another said "DOWN WITH SEGREGATION."

As I stood watching, I suddenly became aware of the large crowds around me. It looked like about 400 spectators to me. Most seemed just curious like me. I wouldn't say that they agreed with the ideas the demonstrators were trying to express, though. A few of the onlookers made some catcalls. As far as I could tell though, no one was causing trouble. The demonstrators themselves were orderly and serious.

A large number of state as well as city police were stationed in the area. I saw perhaps 30 to 35 of them. In spite of their numbers, however, for some reason—not apparent to me—the officers seemed to get panicky. Before I knew it, they had charged into the students and arrested them.

INSTRUCTIONS TO THE JURY

Judge Brown

Ladies and gentlemen of the jury: The defendants in this case are charged with a criminal offense. Under our legal system, a person is innocent until proven guilty beyond a reasonable doubt. This means that the state must place before you enough evidence to convince you, to the satisfaction of your good sense, that such a crime was committed by the persons on trial.

The defendants before this court are charged with the crime of breach of the peace. This crime, according to the statutes of this state, is defined as a "violation of public order and tranquility by any act or conduct inciting to violence or disruption."

The defendants had the rights to freedom of speech and assembly and to petition the government for a correction of injustices. These rights are guaranteed by the First Amendment to the Constitution. The state cannot take them away. If you, the jury, find that the defendants were peacefully expressing their views, that the manner in which they were conducting the demonstration was appropriate, and that they were ordered without reason to disperse, you should find the defendants not guilty.

However, the First Amendment does not deny the state the power to protect the safety of its citizens. Indeed, the state has the duty to act to prevent disorder from occurring. If you find that there was an immediate threat to public peace and safety, that the demonstrators were interfering with the rights of others, or that interference with traffic posed a real danger other than a mere inconvenience, you should find the defendants guilty.

In reaching your conclusions, you may consider the suitability of the place where the demonstration took place. You may take into account the apparent ability of the police force on hand to handle a crowd of that size. You may take into consideration any hostility or friendliness shown by the crowd of spectators. And, finally, you may consider the purpose of the demonstrators.

When making your decision, you should look carefully at what each witness said. Where witnesses disagree, you must decide which witness is reliable.

You should now consider all the evidence.

Foreman of the jury, you should notify me when the jury has reached a verdict.

SUGGESTED READINGS

Archer, Jules. *You and the Law.* Harcourt, 1978. Procedures of the court system are explained as they apply to jurors, witnesses, victims, defendants, and convicts.

Baum, Lawrence. *The Supreme Court.* Congressional Quarterly, 1981. Discusses the history of the Court, its effect on government and society, how judges are selected, which cases are heard by the Court, and the decision process.

Bowen, Catherine Drinker. *Miracle at Philadelphia.* Rev. ed. Little, Brown, 1986. New edition of a classic account of the Constitutional Convention.

Brigham, John. *Civil Liberties and American Democracy.* Congressional Quarterly, 1984. Clear presentation of current themes in civil rights and liberties, with paraphrased Supreme Court decisions.

Cushman, Robert F. *Leading Constitutional Decisions.* Prentice-Hall, 1982. An examination of landmark cases.

Garraty, John A., ed. *Quarrels That Have Shaped the Constitution.* Harper, 1964. Discusses sixteen historic Supreme Court decisions.

Kammen, Michael. *A Machine That Would Go of Itself: The Constitution in American Culture.* Knopf, 1986. Examines the relationship of the American people to the Constitution.

Lewis, Anthony. *Gideon's Trumpet.* Random House, 1964. An account of the prisoner whose letter to the Supreme Court ultimately resulted in the decision that poor people are entitled to counsel.

Lieberman, Jethro Koller. *Free Speech, Free Press and the Law.* Lothrop, 1980. The First Amendment is discussed using controversial Supreme Court cases.

Miller, William Lee. *The First Liberty: Religion and the American Republic.* Knopf, 1986. Studies the constitutional guarantees of religious liberty.

Tribe, Laurence H. *God Save This Honorable Court: How the Choice of Supreme Court Justices Shapes Our History.* Random House, 1985. Discusses the impact of Supreme Court decisions and urges careful selection and approval of justices.

Wishman, Seymour. *Anatomy of a Jury.* Times Books, 1986. A criminal lawyer gives an insider's view of the jury system.

Woodward, Bob. *The Brethren: Inside the Supreme Court.* Simon and Schuster, 1979. The classic expose of the inner workings of the Supreme Court from 1969 to 1976.

Zerman, Melvyn Bernard. *Beyond a Reasonable Doubt.* Crowell, 1981. A lively account of how the jury system works.

GLOSSARY

A

alien a foreigner who is not a citizen of the country in which he or she is living.

allegiance the obligation of loyalty and obedience due to a government in return for the protection it provides.

affirmative action the policy of requiring or encouraging employers to recruit minorities and women in an effort to compensate for past limitations on their opportunities.

amicus curiae a "friend of the court," one who volunteers information to a court on a case in which he or she has no right to appear as a party.

appeal the review by a higher court of a trial held in a lower court on the complaint that an error has been committed.

appellate court a court having the power to hear appeals, review the decisions of lower courts, and reverse lower court decisions when they are in error.

arraignment the part of the process of criminal justice in which the accused is called before the court, informed of the charge, and asked to enter a plea of "guilty" or "not guilty." The accused enters a plea and it is recorded.

arrest the act of depriving someone of his or her liberty, especially as carried out by legally authorized persons.

assault an unlawful attack or threat to do violent physical injury to another person.

at-large election an election held for a state or other government unit as a whole, without that unit being subdivided into voting districts.

B

bail the security (usually money) given for the release of a prisoner to insure that he or she will reappear at the time and place indicated by the court.

Bank of the United States the institution chartered by the federal government to provide sound and uniform currency and to handle financial transactions of the government. (First Bank, 1791–1811; Second Bank, 1816–1836)

Bill of Rights adopted in 1791, the first ten amendments to the Constitution of the United States, guaranteeing the personal rights and liberties of individuals.

blue laws laws designed to regulate activities on Sunday.

booking the process of fingerprinting, photographing, and recording the arrest of a suspect at a police station.

boycott the act of abstaining or joining together with others to stop doing business or otherwise dealing with someone or some group. Boycotts are used as a means of coercion or protest.

breach of the peace an unlawful violation of the public peace and order by disorderly conduct.

bribery the crime of offering, giving, or accepting anything of value to influence the behavior of a public official in the performance of his or her public duty.

brief a written argument prepared by a lawyer to serve as the basis of his or her argument before a court.

bug a tiny, concealed microphone used, primarily with a wireless transmitter, to eavesdrop on private conversations.

burglary the unlawful breaking into and entering of another person's building with the intent to commit a felony.

C

capital crime a criminal offense for which the maximum penalty is death.

certiorari a writ, or order, from an appellate court to a lower court requesting for review a record of the proceedings of a trial.

change of venue a change in the place where a trial will be held.

citizenship the special status, including the rights and responsibilities, of being a member of a nation.

civil case a legal proceeding involving the rights and privileges of an individual citizen.

commerce clause the clause of Article I, Section 8, that gives Congress the power to regulate commerce "among the several states." Over the years, this term has expanded to involve the federal government in a wide range of activities.

common law the body of legal principles based on precedents set by court decisions rather than on statutes passed by legislatures.

communism the economic system in which the factors of production are owned and operated by the government, which determines the type, quantity, and price of goods that will be produced.

concurring opinion an opinion filed by an appeals judge or a justice of the Supreme Court, agreeing with other opinions in the case but giving differing reasons for so concurring.

Confederacy the Confederate States of America, the union of eleven Southern states that seceded from the United States in 1860 and 1861. Jefferson Davis served as President until the end of the Civil War in 1865 when the Confederacy was dissolved.

conscientious objector one who refuses to bear arms or enter military service because of religious beliefs or moral principles.

constitution a body of fundamental principles and laws that describe and limit the government of certain societies. In the United States, federal and state constitutions are written.

contract a legal agreement between two or more parties to do—or not to do—certain acts.

coroner a public officer whose primary function is to hold an inquest into the causes and circumstances of any death that occurs violently, suddenly, or under a cloud of suspicion.

court-martial a military or naval court that brings to trial offenses committed by persons subject to military or naval law.

criminal case a legal proceeding, initiated by the government, to determine the guilt and punishment of a person accused of a crime.

cross-examination in a legal proceeding, the close questioning of one party's witness, by an attorney for the opposite side, to test the truth of the testimony that has been given.

D

damages the sum of money sought by a plaintiff to compensate for the loss or injury he or she suffered through the defendant's unlawful action or failure to act.

de facto in fact; in deed; actually so, but not sanctioned by law.

defendant the accused in a criminal case or, in a civil suit, the party sued by the plaintiff.

de jure according to law; by right; by lawful title.

dissenting opinion a court opinion delivered by one or more judges or justices, disagreeing with both the ruling and the reasoning of the majority opinion; also called the minority opinion.

due process of law all the proper steps required for a fair hearing in a legal proceeding, guaranteed in the United States by the Bill of Rights and the Fourteenth Amendment to the Constitution.

E

equal protection of the laws the constitutional requirement that all persons in like circumstances are entitled to equal treatment by the law and, especially, in legal proceedings.

establishment clause the clause of the First Amendment that forbids the government from making any law about an establishment of religion.

evidence any of the various types of information—including testimony, documents, and physical objects—that a court allows lawyers to introduce in a legal proceeding in order to attempt to convince the court or jury of the truth of their clients' contentions.

exclusionary rule a Supreme Court ruling stating that illegally obtained evidence violates the Fourth Amendment's protection against unreasonable search and seizure and cannot be used in court.

ex parte in law, a term used to describe a legal proceeding undertaken for or on behalf of one side only.

executive order a rule or regulation, having the force of law, issued or proclaimed by the authority of the executive branch of the government.

executive privilege the right of the President and other top executive officials to appear before congressional committees and to withhold information from the courts.

F

Federalist Party one of the first major political parties in the United States. Identified with the theories of Alexander Hamilton, the Federalist Party urged a strong federal government and a loose interpretation of the Constitution.

felony a serious crime punishable by death or imprisonment in a state penitentiary.

free exercise clause the part of the First Amendment that prevents the government from restricting individuals' religious practices.

G

gerrymandering to divide a geographic area into voting districts to give unfair advantage to one party in election.

grand jury a jury of inquiry called to hear the government make charges and present evidence in criminal cases to determine if a trial should be held. When the evidence warrants, the grand jury makes an indictment.

Great Depression the period when the economy of the United States suffered its worst decline. It began following the Wall Street crash of October, 1929, and lasted until the outbreak of World War II. During this period of collapse, business activity fell, banks closed, factories shut down, and as many as 13 million American citizens were out of work.

H

habeas corpus a writ, or court order, requiring that a prisoner be brought before a judge to determine whether the person is being held legally.

I

immigration the coming of an alien into a country in which he or she intends to become a permanent resident.

impeachment a criminal proceeding undertaken against a public official, accusing him or her of some crime or misconduct. Articles of impeachment against members of the executive and judicial branches of the U.S. government are initiated in the House of Representatives and tried in the Senate. If the trial results in a conviction, the official is dismissed.

indentured servant one who signed a contract, or indenture, agreeing to serve for three to seven years in return for passage to America. Once his or her term of service was completed, the servant was freed.

indictment a formal, written accusation of a crime drawn up by a grand jury after hearing the facts of a case.

Industrial Revolution a period of history in which the invention of machines such as the steam engine and the electric motor allowed manufacturers to assemble many workers under one roof. In such factories, laborers used interchangeable parts on assembly lines to mass-produce goods. These could then be sold at cheaper prices than handmade goods to broader and broader markets. In the nineteenth century, these developments influenced the growth of American cities and railroads and resulted in great social and economic changes.

information a written statement accusing someone of committing a crime. Somewhat like an indictment, an information differs in that it is presented by a law officer rather than by a grand jury.

injunction writ, or court order, forbidding the defendant to do a threatened harmful act or directing the defendant to stop such an act already in progress.

inquest a judicial inquiry, usually held before a jury, to determine an issue of fact. One type of inquest is a coroner's inquest, an inquiry into the causes and circumstances of any death that occurs violently, suddenly, or suspiciously.

instructions to the jury the advice or direction that the judge gives to the jury on the law applicable to the case under consideration.

interstate commerce commercial transactions, including the trading of commodities and the transportation of goods and persons, between two or more states.

J

judge a public officer who presides over and administers a court of law. The judge's principal responsibility is to insure that the trials held in court are fair and equitable.

judgment the official decision of the court in civil or criminal cases, ordering that certain acts be done by one or both parties.

judicial restraint the philosophy that judicial decisions should not contradict the wishes of elected members of government unless those wishes clearly violate the Constitution.

judicial review the power or authority of the U.S. Supreme Court to interpret the Constitution, by reviewing and ruling on the constitutionality of orders issued by the President and of legislation passed by Congress and the states.

jurisdiction in law, a court's authority to hear and render judgment on certain kinds and classes of legal cases.

jury a group of citizens, usually twelve in number, selected by law and sworn to investigate certain questions of fact and to return a truthful verdict based on the evidence presented.

justices judges, judicial officials. The U.S. Supreme Court is composed of nine justices—the Chief Justice and eight Associate Justices.

justiciable proper for examination in and subject to the action of a court of justice.

K

kidnapping the unlawful seizure, abduction, and detention of someone, often for ransom. The two essential elements of kidnapping are the false imprisonment and the forcible transportation of the victim.

Ku Klux Klan a secret organization formed in the South after the Civil War to terrorize and intimidate blacks who attempted to assert their rights to equality. The Klan's goal was the re-establishment of white supremacy, both politically and socially.

L

laws the rules and regulations established by society to regulate the conduct of its members.

lawsuit a legal action or proceeding in a civil court; a suit at law or in equity, begun or carried on between two private persons.

libel a false, written or printed statement—published with ill will—that will tend to damage a person's reputation or ability to make a living.

loose constructionist a supporter of a strong central government who advocates the broadest possible interpretation of the powers—both expressed and implied—given by the Constitution to the federal government.

Louisiana Territory the vast area extending from the Mississippi River to the Rocky Mountains and from the Gulf of Mexico to Canada, purchased in 1803 by President Jefferson from Napoleon of France.

M

Magna Charta a charter granted by King John of England to his barons at Runnymede in 1215 laying the cornerstone of English constitutional liberties.

mandamus a writ issued by a court ordering an official to carry out a specified official duty.

martial law overriding rule by state or military forces imposed upon a civilian population in time of war or critical public emergency when normal civil authority has failed to function.

misdemeanor an offense, less serious than a felony, for which the punishment may be a fine or imprisonment in a local rather than a state institution.

Missouri Compromise of 1820 an attempt by Congress to maintain the balance between free and slave states. Under the terms of the act, Missouri was admitted to the Union as a slave state and Maine was admitted as a free state. Slavery was banned in the rest of the Louisiana Territory north of 36°30′.

monopolies a company or group having exclusive control over a particular commercial activity. A company having such control can fix prices higher than a company which must struggle against competition.

Mormons members of the Church of Jesus Christ of Latter-day Saints, founded by Joseph Smith in 1830.

murder the unlawful killing with malice aforethought of one human being by another. When premeditated and deliberate or when committed in conjunction with certain other felonies, this crime is called murder in the first degree. Second-degree murder is the unprovoked and unjustifiable killing of someone when the act is the result of a sudden impulse.

N

naturalized citizen an alien who, by fulfilling certain requirements, becomes a citizen of the country in which he or she is living.

New Deal the bold program for social reform and economic recovery from the Great Depression introduced by President Franklin D. Roosevelt.

nonjusticiable not proper for examination in nor subject to the action of a court of justice.

O

oath a solemn pledge to speak the truth or to perform a certain act faithfully.

original jurisdiction in law, the authority of a court to be the first to hear and decide certain kinds of cases.

overrule to set aside; to reject. A judicial decision may be overruled by a later judgment on the same legal question—either by the same court or by a superior court. The later decision, not the earlier one, is then followed as a precedent.

P

per curiam by the court, an unsigned opinion of the court as a whole rather than of one particular judge. Such an opinion includes no detailed discussion of the legal issues involved.

perjury the willful giving of false testimony while under oath in a judicial proceeding.

plaintiff the party who initiates an action, or lawsuit, against another, who then becomes the defendant.

police powers the general power, or authority, of state governments to protect the health, safety, morals, and welfare of their people. This power is based on the powers reserved to the states under the Tenth Amendment. To some extent, the federal government has evolved similar general powers, based on the commerce clause as well as on the Preamble to the Constitution.

precedent a judicial decision that may be used as a guide in deciding similar cases in the future.

privileges and immunities the basic rights that belong to all citizens of the United States—rights that the Fourteenth Amendment to the Constitution forbids the states to abridge.

probable cause reasonable ground to believe that a crime has been or will be committed, justifying the government's action in searching or arresting a suspect.

probation a type of suspended sentence in criminal cases, granted especially to persons convicted of minor or first offenses. A person on probation can go free, usually under the supervision of a probation officer, as long as he or she remains on good behavior.

Prohibition that period in American history beginning in 1919 with the passage of the Eighteenth Amendment of the Constitution which outlawed the manufacture, sale, or transportation of alcoholic beverages, and ending in 1933 with the repeal of the Eighteenth Amendment by the Twenty-first.

prosecuting attorney the lawyer who conducts the government's case against a person accused of a crime.

Puritan a member of a seventeenth-century religious group who wished to "purify" the Church of England—that is, remove any traces of Roman Catholicism. Some Puritans left England to settle in Massachusetts.

Q

quorum the minimum number of members or officers of a group or organization, usually a majority, whose presence is required to permit the transaction of business.

R

rape the illegal act of forcing another person to have sexual relations.

reapportionment the redistribution of the number of legislators from each electoral district according to population changes.

record the official written report of the proceedings in a legal case.

restrictive covenant an agreement in a real estate, or land, contract that restricts the use of the property to particular purposes—especially to occupancy by members of a particular ethnic group.

robbery the unlawful taking of the property of another, using force or the threat of force.

S

sedition language or action which stirs up discontent or rebellion against the government.

seditious libel written or printed criticism which threatens the security of the government.

self-incrimination testimony or other evidence given by a person, which tends to expose him or her to prosecution for a crime.

sentence in criminal proceedings, the formal judgment in which a judge states the penalty or punishment for a defendant who has been convicted of a crime.

separation of powers key principle organizing the U.S. system of government: the legislative branch makes the laws, the executive branch puts the laws into effect, and the judicial branch interprets the laws and settles disputes over conflicting rights under the laws.

stare decisis the doctrine under which courts decide cases on the basis of precedents—rules established in previous similar cases.

statute a law enacted by a legislature, or lawmaking body.

stop-and-frisk a limited search for concealed weapons conducted by law officers who stop suspects and then quickly run their hands over their clothing.

strict constructionist a supporter of strong state governments who advocates the narrowest possible interpretation of the powers—both expressed and implied—given by the Constitution to the federal government.

subversion action intended to undermine or overthrow something established, such as a government.

suffrage the right to vote in an election, testimony—an oral statement of evidence given by a witness under oath.

supremacy clause the clause of Article VI, Section 2, which states that the Constitution is the supreme law of the land.

T

trial an examination of the evidence and charges involved in a legal case.

U

unconstitutional in violation of the Constitution and, therefore, illegal.

V

vagrant a person who wanders from place to place, homeless and without work.

verdict the formal decision of a jury regarding the facts of a legal case submitted to it at a trial.

W

waiver the voluntary surrender of one's legal rights.

war powers clause the clause of Article I, Section 8, which gives Congress the right to declare war. American Presidents, however, have often sent troops to fight in "undeclared wars."

warrant an order issued by a judge or other authority, directing a law officer to carry out an action, such as an arrest or a search.

wiretap a concealed listening or recording device connected to a communications circuit.

writ a written order from a court, commanding or prohibiting a specified act.

LIST OF CASES

Below is a chronological listing of the cases used in this text, along with the page on which each first appears. Those covered more extensively are cited in boldface type.

1659 The Case of Mary Dyer (p. 13)
1735 The Case of John Peter Zenger (p. 27)
1761 The Writs of Assistance Case (p. 105)
1803 Marbury v. Madison (p. 47)
1810 Fletcher v. Peck (p. 50)
1819 McCulloch v. Maryland (p. 53)
1821 Cohens v. Virginia (p. 50)
1824 Gibbons v. Ogden (p. 54)
1833 Barron v. Baltimore (p. 91)
1857 Dred Scott v. Sanford (p. 71)
1861 Ex parte Merryman (p. 77)
1873 The Slaughter-House Cases (p. 91)
1875 Minor v. Happersett (p. 83)
1879 Reynolds v. United States (p. 17)
1883 The Civil Rights Cases (p. 92)
1896 Plessy v. Ferguson (p. 89)
1914 Weeks v. United States (p. 121)
1919 Schenck v. United States (p. 32)
1925 Dumbra v. United States (p. 105)
1925 Pierce v. Society of Sisters (p. 19)
1925 Gitlow v. New York (p. 34)
1931 Near v. Minnesota (p. 39)
1932 Powell v. Alabama (p. 101)
1935 Norris v. Alabama (p. 101)
1935 Schechter Poultry Corp. v. United States (p. 55)
1936 Ashwander v. TVA (p. 57)
1938 Johnson v. Zerbst (p. 106)
1938 Missouri ex rel. Gaines v. Canada (p. 93)
1942 Betts v. Brady (p. 106)
1944 Korematsu v. United States (p. 78)
1946 Colegrove v. Green (p. 81)
1947 Everson v. Board of Education (p. 18)
1950 United States v. Rabinowitz (p. 118)
1950 Sweatt v. Painter (p. 94)
1950 McLaurin v. Oklahoma State Regents (p. 94)
1951 Dennis v. United States (p. 34)
1952 Rochin v. California (p. 109)
1952 Youngstown Sheet & Tube Co. v. Sawyer (p. 59)
1954 Brown v. Board of Education (p. 93)
1957 Roth v. United States (p. 41)
1958 Trop v. Dulles (p. 123)
1961 Mapp v. Ohio (p. 121)
1961 Scales v. United States (p. 33)
1962 Baker v. Carr (p. 81)
1962 Engel v. Vitale (p. 20)
1963 Edwards v. South Carolina (p. 1)
1963 Gideon v. Wainwright (p. 105)
1963 Abington School District v. Schempp (p. 20)
1964 Wesberry v. Sanders (p. 87)
1965 United States v. Seeger (p. 22)
1965 Griswold v. Connecticut (p. 36)
1966 Miranda v. Arizona (p. 107)
1966 Schmerber v. California (p. 109)
1966 Sheppard v. Maxwell (p. 111)
1967 In re Gault (p. 115)
1967 Afroyim v. Rusk (p. 77)
1967 Berger v. New York (p. 113)
1968 Duncan v. Louisiana (p. 119)
1968 United States v. O'Brien (p. 38)
1968 Terry v. Ohio (p. 117)
1969 Tinker v. Des Moines School District (p. 38)
1970 Welsh v. United States (p. 22)
1970 Oregon v. Mitchell (p. 83)
1971 Phillips v. Martin Marietta Corp. (p. 95)
1971 Bivens v. Six Agents of the Federal Bureau of Narcotics (p. 121)
1971 New York Times v. United States (p. 39)
1972 Furman v. Georgia (p. 123)
1973 Frontiero v. Richardson (p. 94)
1973 Miller v. California (p. 41)
1973 Holtzman v. Schlesinger (p. 61)
1974 Kahn v. Shevin (p. 98)
1974 United States v. Nixon (p. 64)
1976 Gregg v. Georgia (p. 123)
1979 Caban v. Mohammed (p. 98)
1981 Haig v. Agee (p. 67)
1982 Mississippi University for Women v. Hogan (p. 98)
1984 Firefighters Local Union No. 1784 v. Stotts (p. 97)
1984 Immigration and Naturalization Service v. Lopez-Mendoza (p. 125)
1984 Nix v. Williams (p. 125)
1984 United States v. Leon (p. 125)
1985 Dow Chemical Co. v. EPA (p. 126)
1985 New Jersey v. T.L.O. (p. 126)
1985 Wallace v. Jaffree (p. 23)
1986 Local 28 Sheet Metal Workers v. EEOC (p. 96)
1986 Local 93 v. City of Cleveland (p. 96)
1986 Bethel School District No. 403 v. Fraser (p. 43)
1986 Wygant v. Jackson Board of Education (p. 96)
1986 Thornburg v. Gingles (p. 85)
1987 Rotary International v. Rotary Club of Duarte (p. 98)
1988 Hazelwood School District v. Kuhlmeier (p. 43)

INDEX

CREDITS

Cover Design—Dick Hannus

viii-1 From Equal Justice Under Law, courtesy Foundation of the Federal Bar Association photographer, Joseph J. Scherschel

10 (top) Wide World; (bottom) T. A. Rothschild/Stock, Boston

11 (top) Wide World

20 (top left) Stephen Potter/Stock, Boston; (bottom) United Press International

20-21 (background) Charles Moore/Black Star

21 (lower left) Wide World

38 (top left) Claude Zajakowski/American Dental Association; (bottom) B.R. Hopkins

39 (top right) Ralph Crane/Black Star; (bottom right) The Bettmann Archive

50 (top) Wide World; (lower left) Bob Adehnan/Magnum

51 (left) The Bettmann Archive; (right) Culver Pictures

62 (top left) The Bettmann Archive; (background) George W. Cardner

63 (top) Bruce Davidson/Magnum

72 (top left) Burk Uzzle/Magnum; (center left) Lawrence Block; (center) Daniel S. Brody/Stock, Boston; (bottom) Eve Arnold/Magnum

73 (top left) Arthur Schatz, LIFE Magazine © Time Inc.; (center left) Donald Wright Patterson/Stock, Boston; (right) Charles Gatewood